A BOOK ON CAREER MANAGEMENT

How to Study and Succeed

A BOOK ON CAREER MANAGEMENT

How to Study and Succeed

Mukhopadhyay Suvasish

Viva Books

New Delhi | Mumbai | Chennai | Kolkata | Bangalore | Hyderabad | Kochi

Publisher's note

Every possible effort has been made to ensure that the information contained in this book is accurate at the time of going to press, and the publisher and author cannot accept responsibility for any errors or omissions, however caused. No responsibility for loss or damage occasioned to any person acting, or refraining from action, as a result of the material in this publication can be accepted by the editor, the publisher or the author.

Every effort has been made to trace the owners of copyright material used in this book. The author and the publisher will be grateful for any omission brought to their notice for acknowledgement in the future editions of the book.

First Published as You Can Score More in 2006
This revised edition published in 2008
Reprinted 2010, 2011, 2012, 2015, 2016, 2017, 2018

Viva Books Private Limited

- 4737/23, Ansari Road, Daryaganj, New Delhi 110 002
  Tel. 42242200, 23258325, 23283121, Email: vivadelhi@vivagroupindia.net
- 76, Service Industries, Shirvane, Sector 1, Nerul, Navi Mumbai 400 706
  Tel. 27721273, 27721274, Email: vivamumbai@vivagroupindia.net
- Megh Towers, Old No. 307, New No. 165, Poonamallee High Road, Maduravoyal
  Chennai 600 095 Tel. 23780991, 23780992, Email: vivachennai@vivagroupindia.net
- B-103, Jindal Towers, 21/1A/3 Darga Road, Kolkata 700 017
  Tel. 22816713, Email: vivakolkata@vivagroupindia.net
- 7, GF, Sovereign Park Aptts., 56-58, K. R. Road, Basavanagudi, Bengaluru 560 004
  Tel. 26607409, Email: vivabangalore@vivagroupindia.net
- 101-102, Moghal Marc Apartments, 3-4-637 to 641, Narayanguda, Hyderabad 500 029
  Tel. 27564481, Email: vivahyderabad@vivagroupindia.net
- First Floor, Beevi Towers, SRM Road, Kaloor, Kochi 682 018
  Tel. 0484-2403055, 2403056, Email: vivakochi@vivagroupindia.net
- 232, GNB Road, Beside UCO Bank, Silpukhuri, Guwahati 781 003
  Tel. 0361-2666386, Email: vivaguwahati@vivagroupindia.net

www.vivagroupindia.com

ISBN: 978-81-309-1720-7

Published by Vinod Vasishtha for Viva Books Private Limited, 4737/23 Ansari Road, Daryaganj, New Delhi 110 002.

Printed and bound at Replika Press, Kundli, Sonepat, Haryana.

I dedicate this book to
my ideal teacher
Prof D.P. Mazumdar
who taught me how to teach.

"In order to succeed, we must first believe that we can."

—Michael Korda

Contents

Acknowledgements

I am thankful to Ms. Medha Pandit and Mr. S. Sreetilak for the time and effort they spent for me. I sincerely thank my well-wisher Mr. Anil Pandey of Cambridge University Press for his help and cooperation.

I also thank my family members from the bottom of my heart. They sacrificed many evenings, many occasions, many moments, many small and big pleasures of life for me.

MUKHOPADHYAY SUVASISH

Preface

This book is about career management and students' psyche. My experience with the student community motivated me to write this book. My observations and years of experience are presented in this book. Difficulties many students face lightened many dark corners of my mind. Right from the beginning of my teaching career I found many students failing in many subjects. One more thing which I noticed is: students are unable to score more in spite of hard work. I have tried to address the whole student community through this book. It took twelve years to write this book, but the findings are based on my observation since 1990. Whenever I started writing this book, some unseen force stopped me. Since there was a delay, I could include more case studies. There is so much to be done, so much to be seen and so many fresh avenues to be explored. I have tried to keep the book as concise as possible. The title of the book talks of the subject matter of the book. How to study and score more in examinations is discussed in detail, but that is only one part of this book. Apart from that, most of the aspects of a student's life (related to their examination, academics and to some extent personal life) are discussed at length. This book discusses various subjects of interest to the student community. I hope one who assimilates the total content of this book is bound to score more in every field of life. More emphasis is given to the selection of the right vocation. True education should also help the student to discover what they are most interested in. If a student doesn't find the vocation that suits him most, he will find life useless. He will feel frustrated, doing something which he doesn't want to do. True education is to learn 'how to think, not what to think'.

This concept of the famous philosopher J. Krishnamurti is highlighted in this book. The only absolute in the world, Marx said, is change. How the student community has to act with the changing environment is discussed in detail. The whole book is written from my teaching experience. It is written in English so that it can reach a wider audience. I have given even very minute observations gathered over fifteen years of time. I am thankful to those moments which gave me those minute insights. For me teaching is working for the benefit of the students. In my opinion the student community is the most sacred and innocent community. But they are the most neglected community in our country. In a country like India they don't even have basic facilities. Thousands of eyes motivated me to write this book. I saw the despair of many students after failure, and that negativity is the sole cause of my positive outlook, which is the primary motivation behind this book. Very few people are aware of this book except a few students and some very close family members. Whatever happens, nothing can prevent me from thinking in a positive way for the young generation to whom my heart belongs. I could never maintain distance from my students. In different chapters of this book I have tried to relate very simple truths in simpler ways. It is clearly explained how to strive to succeed. I teach to live; I don't live to teach. Thousands of students and their difficulties have taught me many things. What my inner mind has wanted to say for a long time has been crystallized into this book. I tried to ignite the dormant talent of the students with the spark of motivation. I do believe and hope, this book will not only help the students but also the general reader.

Mukhopadhyay Suvasish
professor_sm@rediffmail.com

CHAPTER I

Ten Golden Rules for Every Student

> "Practice is absolutely necessary. You may sit down and listen to me by the hour every day, but if you don't practise, you will not get one step ahead."
>
> —Swami Vivekananda

How true the above lines are! I have felt the meaning of the above lines in every aspect of my student life and teaching life. Initially most of the things seem to be very easy, but when we try to do them, we face many hindrances. There is no alternative to discipline. If a student is really disciplined, success is soon to be his. Creation takes a lot of time, but destruction takes only a couple of seconds. It takes many years to construct a beautiful structure, but an earthquake can ruin it within a couple of seconds. So for every student it takes relentless efforts and a long time to accomplish success. It is more difficult to maintain the position than to achieve it. There are many rules a student should follow. But I have narrowed them down to ten 'golden rules'. Before teaching a subject, I give these golden rules to my students. They are:

1. A student must attend all the lectures of every subject. Due to some unavoidable reason if he misses any lecture he must collect the notes and study them before attending the next lecture. It is mandatory.
2. Give half an hour for each subject every day.
3. A student must possess his own textbooks, calculator, drawing instruments and other necessary things.

4. A student must be consistent with the study routine.
5. He must understand the fundamentals of the subject. For the students of science and engineering, the knowledge of basic mathematics must be absolutely thorough. If required, they may have to refer to the old textbooks of the earlier classes.
6. The students must form a team, so that they can exchange views and thoughts through group discussions. It will help them to develop fluency in English.
7. A student must be positive-minded and optimistic. Never have a surrendering attitude. Don't form any opinion about a subject before reading it.
8. Solve the question papers of the last 3–4 semesters for each subject. It is an examination-oriented approach of study.
9. Don't skip any chapter. Don't treat any portion of the syllabus as optional. Complete the whole syllabus. Don't differentiate between easy and difficult subjects. The quality of the food is important, not the taste. Study all the subjects with equal sincerity.
10. Never be influenced in a wrong way by your seniors and classmates.

Have a higher aim, and you will achieve it by dint of hard efforts coupled with intelligent planning. Have a fellow feeling. Don't have a selfish attitude. Help your friends, and do a good teamwork. If any student follows these ten golden rules, he is bound to succeed.

CHAPTER 2

Different Ways to Make a Teacher Happy

A student should ensure that his teachers are happy with him. The teachers play a major role in a student's life. Unless the teachers are satisfied with a student, he can't be totally successful. Every teacher prefers to see his class in full strength. No teacher of this world likes poor attendance in his class. Now with distance learning, the Internet and e-learning the trend has changed. Students bunk lectures. It is an age-old tradition. Even the teacher who preaches against this bad habit must have bunked some lectures in his college days. With age the mode of thinking changes. So if any student attends all the lectures of a teacher, the teacher naturally becomes happy with him. It is the easiest way to make any teacher happy. But in most of the cases this presence in the class is no more than physical. You have to go one step ahead. Apart from merely attending, if one concentrates and understands the lecture, it will really help him. Very few students talk to their teachers. After listening to the lecture of a teacher if the students share their views with the teacher, it makes him very happy. But getting too close to the teacher is bad too. Over-intimacy is as bad as being defiant. What a teacher likes is participation in his class with obedience and politeness. In spite of being sincere many students become mere sycophants. But sycophancy doesn't pay for a long period. A student with innovative ideas can't be compared with a student who believes in sycophancy. He who is true to himself can make an impression on his teacher's mind.

CHAPTER 3

Avoid Bad Influences

I have seen many students getting influenced in the wrong way by their seniors and classmates. In most of the cases the junior students are influenced in a wrong way by the senior students who have failed. Generally failure converts a student to a negative-minded person. Continuous failure makes one permanently diffident and it becomes a permanent trait. I have often seen students not preparing for a particular subject. When asked, they explain, "The subject is tough. We will take care of it afterwards." It is nothing but procrastination. Without facing any subject one can't get rid of it. If you refuse to face it today, it prevents you from being successful in the examination. If a rabbit closes its eyes on coming face to face with a tiger, will it be spared?

This habit of procrastination is because of the pessimistic attitude of the senior students, and they pass it on to the juniors. Bad habits percolate from one generation to the next generation. Every student requires a very strong mind to refrain from taking an easy way out. Nobody can defeat one unless he permits it. College students are barely out of their teens. They are full of energy, which needs to be diverted in a positive direction with positive thought. Rarely does one talk of self-knowledge. Self-knowledge is the best knowledge.

The students learn one more thing after stepping into a college. That is dishonesty. I have seen very honest students resorting to dishonest means after entering a college because of the influence of bad students. A good student takes very little time to be bad, but a comparatively bad student remains only 'that bad'. The degree of badness doesn't increase with time because his in-built bad habits act as a vaccine. A student should never be dishonest. It is better to be defeated with self-respect than to be successful through dishonesty. Losing with self-respect indicates lack of preparation, but winning by illegal means indicates lack of ethics. Make sure that you are honest to yourself—you are the only person who knows the best about you. None can judge you better than you yourself.

CHAPTER 4

Choose the Right Profession

It is one of the most difficult tasks in a student's life. There are many people who are in wrong professions. Either they made a wrong decision, or there was tough competition. It requires deep introspection and counselling from right people to choose the right profession. If a person is able to select his right profession, he can be very successful even with comparatively less effort. Often we say that success is a result of labour and effort. Always it may not be true. No man is equally skilled in all the professions. Every person is perfect for one unique profession.

Two stages are very important in a student's life. The first one is the phase between his school and junior college, and the second and the most important phase is the period between the junior college and the college life. A student must know what he wants to be. He must strive for that only. A boy who has allergy to mathematics and drawing can't be a successful engineer. Initial indications are always there, but we overlook or ignore them. If any student neglects these indications and goes for a wrong profession, he is bound to fail.

In this regard I would request the parents and senior members of the family not to impose any vocation on a student against his will. They must allow the child to think freely and take the decision on his own. One example will make it clear. A boy whose favourite subject is chemistry is bound to be more successful as a chemical engineer. But in our society people confuse the young minds, and always they force the young minds to go for the stream which offers more money. In the last few years there was a craze for IT (Information Technology). It was observed that students with no interest in 'IT' took it up as their career because of the pressure from their family members. They may earn fat pay packets but their money will corrode their soul. One should not read merely to pass an examination. One should not read only to get a job. If earning money is the only mission in life, why go for education at all? There are many short and easy routes to success.

The juncture between the junior college and college days can be compared to the meandering of a river. This meandering is the most important turn in a student's career. A student must study the subject to which he can relate the most. A wrong profession can be compared to hot water. It may satisfy one's need but can't fulfil his thirst. The guardians, the well-wishers and other family members must be aware of the students' psychology. They must have a probing glimpse into the student's mind. Only proper counselling can help a student in choosing a right profession. If a student gets the right vocation, then only he will succeed in life. Whenever a student gets his choicest stream of study there will be a total unfurling of his creative energy. We should observe the nature and learn a lot from it. If we really think about a particular issue, many doubts will disappear and we will be able to arrive at a proper conclusion. Gradually our dilemmas will dwindle and we will start to make good decisions. Education is the pivot on which the career of a student is mounted. It controls his future.

> "Education is light;
> Education is understanding;
> Education is awareness;
> Education is authenticity."
>
> —J. Krishnamurti

CHAPTER 5

Don't Allow Anybody to Discourage You

It is essential to be strong mentally. We must not allow anybody to discourage us. Most of the people around us are negative-minded, sceptical and cynical. Rarely do we find people with a positive mindset. The people with cynical attitude try to inject negativity in the minds of the young generation. An old mind is like an impenetrable rock, but a young mind is just like a lump of soft clay. We should be extremely careful so that no one can inscribe any wrong message on these fresh young minds. We must not allow depression to grasp them.

A very simple example will make this point clear. A black dot is marked on a white sheet. A negative-minded person can only see the black dot, but a man with a positive frame of mind is able to see a white background. There lies the difference. We should generate positive energy in the atmosphere by looking at the brighter side of every happening. The atmosphere around us is very negative. We see the weeds of doubt, distrust, jealousy and uncertainty around us. It is very difficult to get rid of these weeds. But cleansing them from time to time is possible. If we do that much, a positive and fresh young mind will not be eclipsed by the shadow of negative outlook.

CHAPTER 6

Accept Unexpected Results and Failures

Our life is very long. It is not the journey of a few days or a few months. Each individual has to experience the taste of failure in his life. Only the number of failures or degree of failure varies from person to person. There are many reasons for failure. Always you may not be responsible for your failure. Sometimes they come unexpectedly. In most of the cases failure is confused with academic failures, but there are many other types of failures. Sometimes we get bad results unexpectedly. As an example I would like to share one incident. One of my students named Thomas John had a very good GRE score and the score of his TOEFL was also good. He applied to ten universities of the U.S. He was good-looking, smart, well-mannered and had a good family background. I had recommended him strongly, and he had two more good recommendations from two other faculties. His academic progress was consistently good. In spite of all these John failed in the visa interview. He appeared for the second time and failed again. After this he was disheartened and lost all the enthusiasm and zeal to pursue higher studies in the U.S. After one year again he appeared for the visa interview and failed again. The reason of his failure is still mysterious. He had to accept his failures. Failure is painful, but we can't run away from it. It is advisable to turn that failure into the cause of a success. Never stop after any failure. There is a saying,

"Failure is the only opportunity to begin again more intelligently."

— Henry Ford

The state of one's mind after failure can be compared to the silence of the huddle trees before a storm. One must have the willpower to turn the tearful eyes into the eyes aglow with success.

CHAPTER 7

Language Problem and Solution to It

> "The only thing that stands between a man and what he wants from life is often merely the lack of will to try and lack of faith to believe that it is possible."
>
> —Richard M. Devos

There are students from vernacular medium who face a great difficulty in their professional education where English is used as the medium of teaching. I have witnessed many incidents where students failed to express their feelings because they didn't have the capacity to express their feelings. It really becomes very painful when you are unable to express your inner feelings just for the lack of fluency in English.

I remember one specific incident. On one winter afternoon I was busy reading a technical paper. Suddenly I saw one of my favourite students standing outside my cabin. His name was Salim. He was a very talented boy. He was from the Solapur district of Maharashtra. He was very sound in mathematics, but it was impossible for him to communicate in English. That made him develop an inferiority complex. For this problem there is no panacea or instant solution. Only consistent practice can produce some results. I suggested that he speak in English with his roommates. His roommates were good enough to cooperate with him. Next day Salim came along with his roommates. I told those two boys to help Salim. I advised him to get rid of stammering while communicating in English. It didn't matter if it was wrong, but speed and overcoming shyness were very important. After one month Salim met me again.

Late afternoon light flashed on his innocent face. He looked partially confident. He started communicating in English. It soothed my soul.

CHAPTER 8

Good Handwriting

Handwriting of any student or any person has tremendous importance. There is an expression in English: 'love at first sight'. It is the case with the handwriting. When we see good handwriting, we instantly praise it even before judging the content. There are some things which are to be taken care of right from childhood. Handwriting is one of them. Now there will be a question. If a forty-year-old man finds that his handwriting is bad, what will he do? Will he not try to improve it? The answer is a definite yes. All the time we must remember these two words: 'I CAN'. How much we can is a different question, but certainly 'WE CAN'. There is no doubt about that. Never say 'I CAN'T'. A forty-year-old person may not be able to have a very beautiful handwriting, but definitely with practice, he will be able to write legibly. Practice always pays. Even if improvement is slight, still it is an achievement.

CHAPTER 9

Importance of Discipline

Importance of discipline is appreciated by the disciplined people and felt by the indisciplined. Often we confuse between these two words 'discipline' and 'practice'. Truly speaking, good practice leads to a disciplined lifestyle. Only practice is not enough; emphasis must be given on correct practice. The word 'discipline' comes from 'disciple'. For understanding life you have to understand yourself. A disciplined man knows the values of little things in life. Success is nothing but the integration of small things done in a disciplined manner. Behind every success there is discipline. When we see an athlete winning the gold medal in the Olympics, we applaud him for a couple of seconds. We overlook the rigorous discipline and dedication of four long years that has gone behind an athlete's success. It is easy to walk ten kilometres a day, but it is difficult to walk even half a kilometre regularly throughout the year. Here lies the importance of discipline.

CHAPTER 10

Expose Your Hidden Potential

Generally we are not aware of our hidden potential. It is just like a suppressed stream that needs an outlet. Only motivation by some external agent can help the dormant talents to surface. These great energies are wasted most of the time because they are neglected. Self-motivation is the best motivation. Motivate yourself and use your potential and positive energies. Every human being has some positive attributes, but they get repressed by the cynical remarks of sceptical people. They are camouflaged behind the curtain of failures, anxiety and trauma. Everyone must explore his latent talent and capacity. The factors for proper progress are true self-esteem, belief that you can do it, belief that you deserve it and belief that you can achieve it. For exploring this hidden potential one must know how to think. The mode of thinking is extremely important for true progress. One should not surrender when he faces defeat. The hurdles are the precursors of success. Be defeated, it doesn't matter. Go ahead. Once you win, nobody will count your defeats.

Life is very valuable and one must not waste it. One should never think that it is too late to start anything good. Even a man of eighty years can start a new project. Your age is not a function of years; it is a function of your mental climate. If the mental climate becomes bad, then even a boy of twenty years will be senile, but if the mindset is positive, even an octogenarian will be creative. A creative mind is always young. Perfection doesn't have any end; it is an unending process. Regarding this I would like to quote four lines.

"Good! Better! Best!
Do not rest
Till good be better
And better, best."

—Anonymous

CHAPTER II

Impact of School and College

In a person's life the impacts of his schools and colleges are tremendous. The school has more impact than the college. Every parent wants to admit his/her child to a good school, but how to define a good school? It is very difficult. People think that good school means strict discipline. But I don't agree with them. Very strong discipline corrodes the creativity of a child. Instead of discipline there should be self-discipline. Many students from 'disciplined' schools behave in an undisciplined manner outside their school. This kind of discipline is as good as no discipline. It is like electromagnetism, the moment one switches the supply off, the magnetism is lost.

A school should be a place where the mind of a child can unfold itself; the school should be a place where a child can enjoy. Most schools can be compared to open jails. I have observed many good students very happy in comparatively bad schools. As the competition is not fierce, they get good results and that good result motivates them. If an ordinary student takes admission in a very good school, he is likely to be compared to better students, but if the same student takes admission in a relatively less famous school, then his talent gets a platform. Your tutelage, whether it is a school or a college, must not arrest your enthusiasm. Competition is not bad, but comparison is. It is the highest insult one can receive from the society, relatives and parents. Your school and college should be a place where your mind can unfurl itself, as a brook gushes down a hilly region. If any teacher asks his students what the memorable part of their college days is, their answer should not be 'the holidays'. We should take care of it.

CHAPTER 12

Influence of Friend Circle

A student's life is most of the time influenced by his friend circle. Friend circle acts as a catalyst in a student's life. A 'good friend' and a 'bad friend' both are relative terms. Friendship is a human need. Generally, every human being makes friends with those people who are of his level. Exchange of views and thoughts should take place at the same level. A person who injects good thoughts in your mind is to be treated as a good friend. A true friend is a well-wisher. Most of the time we confuse between a friend and a colleague. In professional life what you get is a colleague, and they are your rivals and competitors. You can find a true friend among your schoolmates. A true friend will never be your competitor. Sometimes we consider a bad colleague as a good friend, and when we are deceived by him, we realize the truth. Under the influence of true friendship the synthesis of good thoughts takes place. But the unbridled youth, most of the time, commits mistakes while selecting friends and that wrong selection leads to progressive decline of moral character and academic career. A friend may offer you alcohol, but when you get addicted to it, he will not save you from it. So students should be very selective while choosing their friends. A good friend may not be able to produce a good result, but a bad colleague will definitely make some bad impact, which will be permanent.

CHAPTER 13

Importance of Communication

Proper and fast communication is essential in today's life. If you don't know how to communicate, then you are an odd man out in this age of fast communication. There are several mediums of communication and the most modern and the most efficient method is the Internet. Email is the most powerful medium of communication. Just imagine one single click of a mouse in the corner of your room sending your message to someone who is thousands of miles away from you.

Good teachers are also good communicators, and a true master does communion. A master is one step ahead of a teacher. Timely communication can save a lot of time. There are several methods of communication. Often we give the address of one friend to another, but along with the address if we give his phone number and email ID, it makes the communication easy. I have seen many people who don't have their email IDs. Some students do have mail IDs but don't use them. If you want to enjoy communication, you have to use the Internet as much as possible. Proper communication is a skill and an art too.

CHAPTER 14

How to Choose Questions

If any student knows how to choose questions to answer in any examination, he can score more. A student should never start his examination with a problem, because if there is any mistake in the calculation, the starting itself gets affected. A student should always start with a comparatively easy question or a theory-type question. In any examination your style of presentation and the way you begin your answers matter a lot. Choice of questions has a tremendous impact on the marks you get. If you choose short notes, you must give the required diagrams and formulae (if it is a technical subject) instead of writing histories. There must be proper sequence in your answers. If the level of preparation of the two students is same, the one who knows how to choose questions will excel.

CHAPTER 15

Time Management in the Examination

Time management in the examination is one of the most important skills of a student. I have observed hundreds of good students who failed to complete their whole papers because they didn't have time to complete the papers. Truly speaking, it is not the lack of time, but the lack of time management. Within the same frame of time another group of students completes the whole paper. But the first group of students fails to do that. A practical example will make it more clear. Imagine that there are six questions in a paper and they are to be answered within three hours. Generally, the students start with a difficult question and for completing the first question they generally take approximately forty minutes. In this way they use time without any planning. By the time they reach the fifth question, they will already have spent more than two and a half hours, and hardly any time remains to answer the last question. It becomes very difficult for the students to write the full answer of the last question. Chance of rechecking of the answers does not arise. The reason is nothing but the sheer lack of time management.

If there are six questions and time on hand is three hours, you need to calculate the time to be given to each question. You can give half an hour time to each question. In this case you should not give more than twenty-five minutes for a question. If it remains incomplete, keep some space and start answering the next question. By one hundred and fifty minutes you will be able to attempt all the six questions. In the last thirty minutes you can give the finishing touches along with the rechecking. Secondly, after answering a question recheck it immediately. It is always preferred and advisable. Please note one thing. Very neat and tidy answers of five questions will bring less marks than comparatively less-tidy answers of six questions. It is essential to attempt all the questions. If you can't, you will be sidelined in this age of cut-throat competition.

CHAPTER 16

How to Tackle Objective-Type Questions

Examination based on objective-type questions is the trend in the modern days. Most of the competitive examinations have an objective-type question paper. Because of increased number of students and cut-throat competition this objective-type examination system has gained immense popularity. There is no descriptive question in these examinations. For these questions the students have to give answers to the point. To prepare for such examinations, a student must have a thorough knowledge of the subject. In this examination it is easy to assess the papers. The evaluation is either manual or computerized, and the judgement is free from any controversy. It is an art to tackle the objective-type question papers. Generally four answers are given for each question. Out of the four options one is correct, and the remaining three options are wrong. Unless one has thorough reading, he will not be able to answer perfectly. So for tackling the objective-type questions one must have thorough knowledge and one must have clarity in his thoughts. Then only will a candidate be able to fare well in an objective-type examination. GRE and GATE are examples, though GATE has some descriptive-type questions too.

CHAPTER 17

How to Tackle Negative Marking

Objective-type examinations can be compared with ODI matches of a cricket tournament. Day by day test matches are losing their popularity. Generally an objective-type question carries multiple choices for the answer. For one question four answers are given, and out of those four answers only one is correct. The students need to be thoroughly prepared for this type of an examination. If a student doesn't know the answer to a particular question then either he can leave out that particular question, or he can tick a particular answer just with a wild guess. This wild guessing is nothing but gambling. It pays at times. Let us take one practical example. Assume there is a question paper that consists of one hundred questions. Let us assume that a candidate knows only the answers to 72 questions out of 100 questions. Now the answers to the remaining 28 questions are not known to the candidate. The candidate has two options. Either he doesn't answer them or makes a wild guess to answer them. In 99.99% cases candidates go for the second option. Out of these 28 questions, for some questions the correct option is 'a', for some correct option is 'b', for some correct option is 'c', and for the rest of the questions the correct option is 'd'. Let us assume that the candidate who doesn't know the answers to 28 questions decides to attempt them just by wild guess. In that case he will do the tick-marking at random. He may score some marks, because according to the law of probability all the attempts can't be wrong. Usually they tick nearly 30% to 40% correct answers. So just by gambling a student gets correct answers of 9 to 10 questions out of 28. Now if it is assumed that he has answered 10 questions correctly just by wild guessing, the number of correct answers will be 82 (72 + 10) and the last ten answers are the resultant of gambling. But gambling must not be a part of an examination. Gambling is a breach of the examination ethics.

Paying attention to negative marking is also a very important factor while appearing for an examination that is based on objective-type questions. In some examinations it is 1: 4, in some cases it is 1: 2 and in a very exceptional case it is 1: 1. When the weightage is 1:4, if any candidate gives four wrong answers, mark for one correct answer is deducted. So when negative marking scheme is applied, it becomes very risky for a student to answer any question by guess. If at all any candidate gambles, he must have some logic to support it. The earlier example shows that 28 questions remain unanswered. In this condition if any candidate does tick-marking at random (it is assumed that for some questions he ticks option 'a', for some questions option 'b', for some questions option 'c', and for the rest option 'd') he is supposed to score some marks. But that is not a judicious attitude. In this case if you want to answer the remaining questions, then you should tick only one option. It may be (a), (b), (c) or (d). If you give tick-marks only to (c) option 28 times for all the 28 questions, then definitely you will score some marks, because out of 28, for some questions the correct option must be (c). If any candidate adopts this method, then he will not be a loser in spite of negative marking. Let us assume that the ratio of negative marking adopted is 1:2 (generally it is 1:4) and the candidate gave correct answers to 10 questions and incorrect answers to 18 questions. For the 10 correct answers he will get 10 marks and for the 18 incorrect answers he will lose 9 (18 X ½) marks. Still he gains one mark. If the ratio of the negative marking adopted were 1:4, then he would have more benefit. This is a case study I conducted a few years ago. This is the proper method to tackle negative marking. Whether to adopt this method or not depends on a candidate's personal code of ethics. It is observed that people with true ethics never go for gambling.

CHAPTER 18

Learn from Mistakes

Everyone must learn from one's own or others' mistakes. It is costly to learn from one's own mistakes. Learning from a mistake means not to repeat the same mistake. Behind every mistake there is a cause, and learning means to discover the actual cause behind the mistake. He is an intelligent man who learns from his own mistake, but the person who learns from others' mistake is a wise man. The span of life is too small, and within this small span if every time we keep on learning from our own mistakes, then it will be at the cost of our life. We must remember one thing. Failure is not the ultimate end, but only a delay. Whenever any failure occurs due to any mistake, we become the victims of frustration. If the same mistake is repeated, the result is repetition of the failure. So when there is a failure, we should accept it and admit it too. We must not be depressed. We must learn from the failure and we must be careful so that it doesn't repeat in future. We must not blame others. Generally when we face any failure, we shift the responsibility to others and when we get success, we want to take the complete credit. This fact is observed since the dawn of human civilization. This is an ingrained quality of human character. Here I want to share an interesting incident. In the year 1999 one of my students failed in the GATE examination due to lack of time management. He met me and I had counselled him for hours together. He could realize his weak points. He was a good student, but he didn't know time management. In 2000 again he appeared for the GATE examination, and he was one of the top rankers of the country. What a change! The change took place because he had learned from his mistakes. In 1999 also he would have passed by securing a marginal score, but in 2000, due to proper counselling and introspection, the candidate was one of the top rankers of GATE in India.

CHAPTER 19

How to Face Interviews

Interview is an integral part of academic career, service career and professional life. Giving a good interview is an art. It is the ultimate presentation of a person in front of the experts. Often we forget one thing: what we learn in three to four years is judged within merely 15–20 minutes. That much time is enough to judge a candidate. Only one grain of rice needs to be checked to see whether the rice is properly boiled or not. It is the case with a candidate. An interview is a part of our career; and nervousness is a part of an interview. Nowadays because of growing population (mainly in the developing countries and third world countries) and cut-throat competition, the job markets have shrunk. In the countries where per capita income is small, there are too many candidates for a single job. When the applications are collected and the ratio is calculated between the number of applications and the number of posts, it turns out to be very imbalanced. In any interview if you become too hopeful, it will cause too much of tension and unrest within you. Never be defensive; never play only to avoid defeat. Be smart and take care of your attitude. You shouldn't be arrogant or aggressive in the interview. Many things should work together for a good interview. There are some tips given below:

i. Your dress should be clean, and your get-up should be appealing.
ii. You should use perfume, but don't use too much.
iii. Talk slowly but clearly.
iv. Be a good listener.

v. Have patience, and your body language should not indicate any uneasiness.
vi. Give answers to the point and be brief.
vii. Be prepared and confident about your achievements listed in your resume. Have all the records of your achievements with you.
viii. Have good fluency in English.
ix. Use the words like 'sorry', 'thank you', 'beg your pardon' at proper places.
x. Don't be too hopeful and excited.

These are some essential tips to make you successful in an interview.

CHAPTER 20

Motivate Yourself

In this world people are very busy and nobody is there to motivate you. Either they don't have the wish to motivate you or they don't have the time. In this world of rat race even the parents are too busy, and they can't give the required time to their children. Due to lack of motivation many young minds become unproductive. They start underestimating themselves. Edward L. Kramer has said:

> "Never underestimate yourself. You are the most important thing in this universe."

In this cruel atmosphere if a young mind dies, nobody bothers for it (except a few family members and a few friends). Even the family members stop being considerate after a couple of months. Your grief is absolutely yours; the external world has neither the intention nor the time to share it. In this place you are requested to do self-counselling, and it can extract the highest output out of you. Never have the fear of failure. Fear of failure is more harmful than failure itself. You must have high self-esteem. You must motivate yourself and it must be a continuous process. One-time motivation doesn't stay for a long time. It loses its effect very quickly. You have to be self-made, and all the time you must say to yourself, 'I CAN DO IT.' There was a famous psychiatrist who cured many dreaded diseases just with the help of positive thoughts. Negative thought itself is death. Motivation, and especially self-motivation, is the gateway to success. A man with positive thought rarely becomes tired even after a tiring work schedule. On the other hand, a man with negative thoughts becomes tired even after minimal work. This happens because of the difference in the states of mind. A positive mind continuously supplies energy while a negative mind can be compared with a black body. Black body absorbs energy. (I cannot describe a black body in detail. It is studied under the subject of 'Heat Transfer' in Mechanical Engineering.) Unless your mind is tired, you can't be tired. For the negative-minded people their mind is tired even before they start working. Self-belief is another aspect of self-motivation. There is a saying,

> "In order to succeed, we must believe that we can."
>
> —Michael Korda

How true it is! If you have self-confidence, no external resistance can prevent you from getting success. But if you lack self-confidence, even the slightest difficulty may become the cause of your failure. A green jackfruit can be softened by blows, but not made sweet, because sweetness is an internal matter and that can't be imposed. One must be internally driven to be a successful person. You must have some commitments. It will give birth to excitement and the ultimate result will be motivation. If you say to yourself, 'NOTHING IS IMPOSSIBLE', then 99% of the difficulties will vanish. Life is precious. No one should waste it. For creating fire we require only a spark. Motivation is that spark. Stand in front of a mirror, look at yourself and just say, "I Can."

CHAPTER 21

How to Develop Your Personality

> "There are millions of ways to have a personality, but there is only one way to have individuality."
>
> — Osho

Personality is a very important parameter in a person's life. An educated person without personality is bound to fail in his personal as well as professional life. Individuality is nothing but personality focused in a direction. There are certain factors which control your personality. Some of them are given below:

i. The way you talk
ii. The way you walk
iii. The way you dress
iv. The way you eat
v. The way you share your feelings and emotion
vi. The way you react to silly things or silly jokes
vii. The way you react to guests, strangers and visitors
viii. The way you react to failure
ix. The way you react to some financial gain or benefit
x. The balance of your temper

There are many other points but these are some of the very important points which determine the personality of an individual. A man with a good personality is never afraid of silly things and has a fighting spirit in the time of difficulty. A man with a good personality is not afraid of anybody. The mission of a man with conviction is: 'Never surrender, make yourself do it.'

With a good personality it becomes easy to survive in this world and the possibility of getting noticed among others is much higher. A qualified man without any personality can only be compared to a joker. People with a strong personality never compromise. They never do those things for which the mind doesn't give a signal. You must have a good personality, but good personality must be accompanied by creative and positive thoughts. Good personality and flight of positive thoughts are complementary. They together create great things. A man with good personality never gives in to a negative mentality. Negative mentality is more corrosive than negative results, because negative result is nothing but the by-product of a negative mind.

CHAPTER 22

How to Tackle Stress

"Life is a challenge" – Meet it.
"Life is a struggle" – Fight it.
"Life is a sorrow" – Overcome it.
"Life is a gift" – Accept it.
"Life is a chance" – Utilize it.
"Life is a journey" – Complete it.
"Life is a duty" – Perform it.
"Life is an opportunity" – Take it.
"Life is a problem" – Solve it.
"Life is a goal" – Achieve it.

—Anonymous

There are many things to do in life, why waste it by getting stressed? Nowadays in city life stress is an unavoidable part of life, and it corrodes the fibre of life. How to control stress? It is an important question. Stress is a problem which can't be eliminated, but can only be controlled.

At first we must see what can happen if we don't take stress. Secondly we must see why we take stress. One of the most important reasons of stress is target-oriented job or work-schedule, and the second reason is cheap competition. Stress and depression can be compared to two sides of the same coin. Charles Darwin said, "It is the struggle for existence" and Bertrand Russell said, "It is the struggle to outshine others." In today's world the words of Russell are more applicable. Cheap competition leads to tension and tension gives birth to stress.

It can be very clear with a simple example. One of my friends used to stay in a posh locality of Pune, and he was provided with a very comfortable and fully furnished flat by his company. He had a dazzling white Maruti car. Whenever

I visited his home, I found him morose and never saw him driving his car. Once I asked him and got a peculiar reply. His wife was very unhappy. Because in their society they were the only family to possess a small car and all the other members had the luxury cars like Honda, Accent, Lancer and Mercedes. What an inferiority complex! This is sheer lack of proper education. So if you just peep into your mind, you would see that the reasons of most of the stresses are meaningless. Proper counselling is essential. Only medicine can't control this stress. Only scratching the surface of the problem will not give a positive result. One has to go deeper into it. Many times stress originates due to overwork and target-oriented job. There you have to change the pattern of your working. Truly speaking, stress and greed have a linear relationship. They are directly proportional to each other. Often we say, "Look, how happy a farmer is!" But we never look into the lifestyle of a farmer. He has nothing to lose. I don't mean that one should sit idle, but what I want to say is, "Get rid of cheap and meaningless competition." We must work hard, because smooth seas do not make skilful sailors. Along with hard work we must possess a soft and clear mind. A mind which is already hardened with pride, jealousy, bias and cheap competition can produce nothing else but stress.

CHAPTER 23

Essential Qualities of a Student

For a good result a student must possess some basic qualities. Every student wants a good result, but very few want to work hard. There is no substitute for hard work. Hard work should be combined with a proper method. If any student takes care to develop the following attributes, he will certainly be academically and professionally more successful than others, and he will be on a higher plane which is beyond the reach of the average students. The qualities which a student must possess are given below.

i. Hard-working nature
ii. Punctuality
iii. Good imaginative power
iv. Good power of expression
v. Attentive nature
vi. Good reading habit
vii. Flaming enthusiasm
viii. Noble ambition
ix. Politeness
x. Sincerity
xi. Self-discipline
xii. Curiosity
xiii. Creativity
xiv. Regularity

A student should have these essential qualities. Apart from these there are many other qualities. I see many students doing selective studies, always keeping a few chapters for option. Let me give a clear idea about chapters left for option. Chapters in option means those chapters which are not even touched by the student. That is an unpardonable offence. Just imagine if a student of medical science leaves liver and heart for option (because questions from liver and heart were there in the pervious examination, and they are unlikely to repeat) and prepares for other organs, what will be its impact? A candidate who doesn't even prepare for his examination will never read these topics in future. What kind of a doctor will he become? If any patient with liver or heart ailment comes to him, will he refuse to treat him? The answer is a big 'no'. What will that doctor do then? He will knowingly give wrong treatment and the innocent patient will suffer. His ego will not let him admit that he doesn't know his subject properly. From this example one simple inference can be drawn. It is a crime to study selectively, and no student should do that, and the students of professional courses should be more serious. No student should ignore any doubt, because it means he has remained blank in that particular area. Every student must get his doubts cleared. Attention is important. I say to my students, "If you have confusion in your mind due to some doubts, focus on the confusion, get it cleared and then be attentive."

Don't let your doubts hinder your understanding. Get them clarified so that you can be attentive to the new concepts of other chapters. A student should not aim to pass only. Don't try to get rid of the examination. Normally the aim of a common student is to get rid of the examination at any cost and to get a job. That is an absolutely wrong attitude. A student should feel involved while studying his subjects. The student community must not forget that student life is the most important stage of their life, and the attitudes, works and activities in their student life will pay them in their future. No student should waste his student-hood by involving himself in activities such as politics, addiction to drugs or alcohol and meaningless gossiping. These three habits are very common in hostel life. Someone may raise a question, "Is it bad to involve oneself in politics in student life?" I would say, "It is definitely bad." This is my personal opinion. From my own life and experience I can say with authenticity that I have seen many such students. They tried to change the society but they couldn't even make their own life comfortable. They simply wasted the precious years of their student-life by involving themselves in politics. They were just used by the political leaders. They can be compared to a sugar cane before the extraction of its juice. The political leaders extract their full energies. They are totally used by the politicians and by that time their college life comes to an end. By that time these innocent young victims are exhausted and the hope to do anything oozes out of them. They become only the silent spectators.

If you are a hostel inmate, never allow others to make your room the common room of the wing. Work hard, go ahead and achieve your esteemed goal. Who says you are an ordinary person? Always believe that you are unique. There is nobody just like you.

CHAPTER 24

Physical Attendance in a Class

In my teaching life I have seen and counselled thousands of students. I have come into contact with hundreds of teachers. Students' physical attendance in the classes has tremendous importance in the student–teacher relationship. I feel that in our country in most of the cases physical attendance is another name of physical arresting. But if a student's attendance is marked less in a particular subject, he falls out of the teacher's favour. Only by being physically present in a teacher's class can you bring a metamorphosis in the teacher's attitude. Suppose a teacher has a wrong idea about you. Just go on attending all his lectures, and at the end of the term his idea will definitely change. If you just become sincere, it is enough.

I remember one incident which took place nearly fourteen years back. In one of my practicals in a winter morning I found a student shivering in one corner of the laboratory. Initially I thought it was because of cold. Afterwards I came to know that the boy had 103°F temperature. In spite of that he was physically present. Till date I can't forget that incident. It made a permanent impression on my mind, which I will remember till the end of my life.

CHAPTER 25

First Lecture of Any Subject and Its Importance

The first lecture of any subject can be compared to the first year of a child's life. If any student misses the first lecture of any subject, he loses the essence of that subject. The first lecture is something different than the other lectures. I can speak about the first lecture which I give at the starting of each semester. My first lecture contains many things apart from the basic subject for which the lecture is given.

Always I give maximum importance to the first lecture of every subject. If a teacher fails to attract the students' attention in his first lecture, probably he will fail for ever. For any class (whether it is a nursery class or postgraduate class) the first impression of the teacher proves to be the last impression. However erudite a teacher may be, he must come close to the students. He has to enter the young hearts and place a love for the subject in those young hearts. Whenever the students don't enjoy the first lecture of a subject, the academic activities of the students come to a halt. If they persist at all, they are carried on at a very sluggish pace. For every student it is mandatory to attend the first lecture of every subject. If they fail to do so, they will be unable to catch the thread and may lose interest in the subject.

CHAPTER 26

First Chapter of Every Subject

The first chapter of every subject is of immense importance. Generally the students don't give adequate time for understanding the first chapter of any subject. For completing the syllabus at an early date they go on with a hectic speed with partial understanding of the basics of any subject. The basics or the fundamentals of any subject lie in its first chapter. Without enjoying the starter, you can't enjoy a good dinner. Similarly, without understanding the first chapter, you can't understand a subject. Whenever a subject is theoretical, there can be a question of partial understanding, but when a subject is mathematical, then the term partial understanding is not applicable. For mathematical subjects either the understanding can be hundred per cent or zero per cent. Another important thing is that mathematical subjects are interlinked. Whenever you want to assimilate Advanced Hydraulics, your idea of Basic Hydraulics must be clear. Whenever a child doesn't get proper nutrition after his birth, he suffers throughout his life. Even in the later life if he is given good food and nourishment, his growth and development become relatively poor. Care must be taken at the beginning. It is the case with any subject. It is essential to have clarity in your thoughts. If the first chapter of any subject is not clear to a student, then he will not be able to have mastery over that subject in spite of relentless efforts taken later. If it is not achieved, the student has to pay the penalty in the future. In understanding a subject there can be no shortcut. What can the teacher do? He should give adequate time for having proper understanding of the fundamentals of his subject. Now in this age of Information Technology downloading from the net is a shortcut approach, but it is not a panacea. No one can learn surgery or welding from the Internet, it requires thorough practice. I do believe my readers will agree with me.

CHAPTER 27

Completing the Whole Syllabus: A Necessity

To complete the whole syllabus is extremely essential for a student. It is important for examination as well as for knowledge. Completion of syllabus can be compared to a complete balanced diet. Nowadays there is a trend to leave some chapters for option. Already I have discussed this in detail. Assume there are ten chapters, and in the examination the number of questions may also be ten. Generally, from each chapter one question comes, and the student has to attempt six questions in all. As a reference, I am using the pattern of a question paper in an engineering subject at the University of Pune. Each question carries approximately 16 marks. There are two sections. Each section consists of 50 marks. In both the sections the candidate is supposed to attempt three questions out of five. Generally, one question is set from one chapter, and there are sub-questions under the main question. It indicates that if any candidate completes 60 per cent of the syllabus, he can attempt all the questions. Generally, for the entire subject the whole syllabus is divided into ten parts. The candidate is supposed to answer six (three + three) questions out of ten (five + five) questions. Is this good? Definitely it is bad.

Nowadays students do selective studies. They go through the recent question papers. By wild guessing they prepare for only some chapters. A student of medical science can get his medical degree without studying his subjects in depth, but will he not be a criminal with a certified license? The pattern of questions should be such that it must compel the candidates to cover the whole syllabus. Unless you complete the whole syllabus, you can't be confident. This will create diffidence within you. The authority should be strict enough to take care so that there can't be any shortcut to studies. Nowadays we don't compromise with anything. In a dinner if you are not given the soup and ice cream, will you like it? Definitely the answer will be 'no'. There can be dinner without soup and ice cream. It will satisfy your appetite, but not give you the desired enjoyment. Similarly, unless you complete the whole syllabus, you can't get a command over that subject. Completion of syllabus is the prerequisite for going ahead. Only the good students can beautify the academic landscape of this world.

CHAPTER 28

How to Adjust with Hostel-mates and Roommates

Many students have to stay in a hostel during the span of their education. In most of the hostels one has to share his room with more than one person. Environment of the hostel plays a major role in a student's mind. Whenever one stays in a hostel, one must have a healthy relationship with his roommates and other inmates of the hostel. If he can't adjust with the hostel atmosphere, he will be cornered, and it will invite complications. Adjustment doesn't mean excessive mixing with one's friends. It means mingling with everybody, but keeping some distance. Adjustment is the key word for being successful in public life. Wherever you stay, if you possess positive thought and helping nature, everybody will like you. Never leave positive thoughts. Food nourishes the body and positive thoughts nourish the soul. From my own experience I do agree that sometimes one may face difficulties in hostel life. In hostel you have to adjust with various kinds of human beings. While living in the hostel you should neither be selfless nor selfish. If you become selfish, friends will abandon you, and you will be confined to your own company. In that case your mental growth will stop. On the other hand, if you become selfless, your friends will exploit you, squeeze you and throw you after use. So you have to be practical. When I shifted to hostel from home after admission to the engineering course, one of my brother's friends told me, "Enjoy with everybody, but don't allow others to use your room as a common room." Sometimes it becomes difficult to adapt to the curves of life, but then you can't stop. You may have to judiciously apply the brake of your mind. If you can adjust with your hostel-mates, you can acquire managerial qualities right from your student life without learning management. There are many famous managers who haven't had any formal training in management. Management is basically proper and timely application of your common sense. An experience of hostel life for a couple of years is required for the proper mental growth of every person.

CHAPTER 29

Why Bunking Lectures Is to Be Avoided

Bunking of lectures is a very common trend nowadays. Gradually the student community is becoming less and less interested in attending lectures. What is the reason behind this? If we look for the cause, many unwanted things may come to surface. Whenever a student does not attend the lectures, there can be basically two reasons. Either he doesn't like the subject, or he doesn't like the way of teaching. I am keeping this point aside for the time being. Nowadays with distance learning and e-learning, students can get better material. Still they can't avoid the conventional classroom teaching. If the teacher is good, he requires nothing more than the blackboard and chalk, and automatically he attracts the students.

Nowadays 75 per cent attendance is compulsory for a student to be granted a term, but this attendance is nothing but physical arresting. After bunking a lecture students give many false excuses. They don't dare to confess the actual reason. Here is a joke about a student who lied to his principal.

"Do you believe in life after death?" the principal asked a student. "Yes Sir," replied the student. "Fine! that explains everything," said the principal. "About an hour after you left for the funeral of your grandfather yesterday, he came to the college to meet you."

Another reason why students bunk classes is bad teaching. This joke is about that.

One professor asked another professor, "How is your

class?" "Terrible. Even the students who used to sleep in the class have stopped coming," replied the professor.

I agree with the grievances of the student community. Still I suggest that the students don't bunk lectures. Whatever the subject and whoever the teacher, the lectures must be attended. It always pays. If one is regular in the class, he won't feel out of tune. Every teacher likes the students who are regular in his class. In this world people rarely accept their weak points, but always point out those of others.

It was 1990. I had just joined the College of Engineering and Technology, Jalgaon. One day I didn't get time to iron my shirt. In my department one of my colleagues asked me, "Have you not ironed your shirt?" He was a typical cynic, and he himself never used to wear ironed and clean dress. But these are the people who observe everybody and judge everybody. Their judgement is nothing but criticism. Most of the society is made of this type of people. If you pass ten times they will not congratulate you, but if you fail even once they will ask you the result in spite of knowing it. They are the typical depressed persons with a wicked mindset.

Even a very bad teacher likes a boy who is regular in his class. In my own teaching life I have seen many students bunking lectures for various reasons. Most of the reasons given by them were nothing but lame excuses. Bunking of lectures is not only a disease, but a contagious one too. If you see your roommate bunking lectures, you may be tempted to do the same under his evil influence. We are always influenced by the evil things very quickly. Generally after bunking the lecture either the students gossip in the canteen or indulge in some other activities. Those activities are seldom creative. All of us should take this issue seriously and try to bring about a change in our attitudes.

CHAPTER 30

How to Use Your Books

If any student knows how to use his books, he knows ninety per cent of the art of learning. Generally, most of the students go for more than one textbook for each subject and rarely do they concentrate on one book. From my experience of teaching I would suggest that they follow just one standard textbook for each subject. In the semester pattern the students hardly get sixteen weeks' time for preparation and within those sixteen weeks they go through four to five subjects. So if the students follow only one textbook for each subject it will save their time. Usually the owner of any book uses it less and others use it more. In any book the proper understanding and assimilation of the first chapter is very essential.

Some people do markings in the book, regarding this I prefer to be non-committal. It is left to the reader. If anybody thinks that marking in the book helps him, he is free to do that, but too much of marking leads to confusion.

There is a trend not to buy the books, and if at all they buy, they go for second-hand or even third-hand books to save money. How much can a student save by going for a second-hand or third-hand book? It is a legitimate question. While buying other things we never compromise; then why this economy only for the books? It clearly indicates that students give secondary treatment to their academics. For a student, education must be the first preference. Generally it is difficult to consult the reference books within the small span of time, but a student must see the reference books.

I want to share one of my experiences with my readers. There was an illiterate man. Every day he used to visit a teashop, and he used to go through the newspaper for half an hour. One day a waiter couldn't resist his curiosity. The waiter knew that the man was illiterate. The waiter candidly asked him, "What do you read? You are illiterate!" The man smiled and replied, "My boy, I may be illiterate, but it doesn't require any literacy to see the pictures in a newspaper. And I learn so much from these pictures and photographs." The waiter was surprised by this logical reply.

Similarly, if any student doesn't get time to consult the reference books, let him have the basic idea of the reference books. Let him know the names of the books and let him see the covers of the books. It also pays. Because others don't even do this much. In any interview even if you are able to say the names of three to four reference books of a subject along with the name of the authors, it impresses the interviewers. One should jot down all the important points and formulae (subject wise) before the examination. There is a very valid reason behind using one textbook. Most of the time notations and symbols vary from book to book. So students should use only the notations and symbols which are recognized and accepted at the international level. Finally, when the question of recommending a textbook comes then the students must follow the advice of the concerned subject teacher.

CHAPTER 31

Textbooks and Reference Books

At undergraduate level the role of reference books may not be that important. If a candidate gets time to go through the reference books, it reinforces his knowledge. Rarely is it possible for a student to go through the reference books. But reading them is very useful for enhancing the knowledge. If anyone just does one per cent extra work than his fellow workers, he may achieve a great difference in the result.

A standard preparation and a good preparation can be compared to French fries without sauce and with sauce. Consulting reference books does add flavour to the preparation of a candidate for examination. Role of the textbook is 90% and role of reference books is 10%. In post-graduate classes, the role of reference books becomes more important. Truly speaking, in post-graduation there can't be a single textbook for any subject. Students have to consult reference books to get a comprehensive idea about their subject.

CHAPTER 32

How to Use the Library

How to use a library is a very relevant question. A library has a bafflingly wide range of books. The Internet and e-learning have in fact reduced library usage. But to develop a good reading habit and expand one's knowledge, one must regularly visit the library. A library is like a spring under pressure about to burst with unlimited force. One needs to tap the unbounded knowledge in a library. You may have books at home, but you cannot create the atmosphere of a library. Everything cannot be bought by money. The academic aroma of a good library is a unique thing. A student should visit the college library at least twice a week. You can have your own convenient time for visiting the library. It can be morning, afternoon or even evening. But the best time to go to the library is the morning. In the morning you have fresh energy to read.

CHAPTER 33

Managing Your Sleeping Hours

It is very important for a student to manage his sleeping hours. Students tend to sleep longer when the examinations are away. Then they are not under any kind of pressure of study. But as the exam season nears by, they begin to burn the midnight oil. During the PL (preparation leave) many of them get to sleep no more than 3–4 hours a day. Those who stay in the hostel usually sleep and wake up late. If it is a holiday, many wouldn't leave the bed before lunchtime.

There are various opinions about how long one should sleep. Some would say eight hours. For some it is seven hours. Yet some others are happy with only six hours. There can be a fourth group that maintains that even nine hours of sleep is insufficient. But it all depends on when you go to bed. If one sleeps very late, he may feel tired even after twelve hours of sleep. But if you go to bed at around 10 p.m. just seven hours of good sleep can prepare you for a fresh day.

In the examination season, especially between two papers, students sleep less. This is not advisable. Disturbing your pattern of sleep will cause stress, indigestion and a host of other problems. I have seen students sitting totally flustered in the examination hall because they haven't slept the night before. If you don't give proper rest to your mind and body, they will betray you at the most critical time. When you try to manage everything in the eleventh hour, efficiency will suffer. Students should have regular sleeping hours and a balanced sleep pattern. You can call this effective 'sleep management'.

A few among us would stay in bed even when they don't have a mind to sleep. This is called lethargy. One can wake up a man who is sleeping, but not one who pretends to sleep. Go to bed only when you really want to sleep, and the nap in the afternoon is best avoided. Old habits die hard. But you can surely get into a new routine with gradual and conscious effort. Those who do not wake up on time will be woken up by failure. A life without discipline can make an average man of an intelligent man. Conversely, an ordinary man with average intelligence but great discipline will go places. So why not make the decision to stay disciplined about your sleeping hours? It really pays, though initially it is difficult to adopt.

CHAPTER 34

Why Purchase the Books

On one autumn afternoon I was sitting in my laboratory; dappled sunlight was filtering through the dark green trees. Suddenly one of my students approached me for some textbooks. He was quite well-off and belonged to a rich family. I asked him why he didn't purchase the book. I didn't have any intention of not giving the book. I only wanted to know why he hadn't purchased it, because he could well afford it. His reply made me sad. He answered, "Why purchase? I require it only for two weeks. Throughout the semester most of the boys don't need books. I require it only for the PL (preparation leave) of two weeks. I don't want to waste money." I was really shocked by his reply. At the same time I appreciated his candour. He was from a rich family, but his attitude towards education was reflected in his answer. Students spend on everything else but rarely do they spend on books. This is a very negative practice. If one can afford them, one must have his own books. Why borrow from others? I have seen many students purchasing second-hand books (if at all they purchase). When for all other things your preference goes for the new things, why not for the books? The answer is very simple: you don't have any love and attachment to your subject. Most of the students want a degree only to get a job, and the moment they complete their education, they forget all they've learned. This is not correct. Your whole life depends on your education. Why not give it the first priority? A person, whether he is a clerk or chief engineer, generally wants his degree or degrees for further achievement in his life. When the success of your life largely depends on your education, why stay away from it? If you are a cook, you are supposed to be attached to your kitchen. If a farmer hates his plough, he can never enjoy farming. Similarly, if a student wants to skimp on books, he can't be considered a student.

CHAPTER 35

Don't Empty the Bin

Some students are only interested in scoring marks. They mug up their lessons quickly and forget them faster. This is observed in every school. A student of 8th standard forgets all he learned in the 7th standard. The students and parents seldom give any value to the portions covered previously in the junior classes. They often forget that the concept of today is based on the acquired knowledge of the past. Earlier classes are the foundation for later classes. For a bad student, the previous class is like a waste bin. A better student treats it as his reference for his present study. Some throw away old textbooks and notebooks because they do not want 'garbage' in their house. Others sell off their books even before the results come out. A few books will not make your house dirty. This is an attitude students and parents have to change. You need to refer to old books whenever you face any doubt. Selling the old books will kill even the habit of getting your doubts cleared.

I have preserved most of my notebooks from my engineering days. There may be a hundred good textbooks, but the notes a good teacher dictates have no substitute. They contain the teacher's experience in miniature form. Remember that a man is often what a teacher makes him.

CHAPTER 36

On Taking Notes

There is no fixed method of taking notes. Every teacher doesn't give notes. You may find it difficult to listen to the lecture while taking notes. When you enjoy a good lecture you cannot jot down the points, and if you begin to jot down, you can't enjoy the lecture. You cannot eat and drink together. But you can have a few sips after a few mouthfuls. In the same way, do enjoy the lecture and take notes of only important points. You can expand on it on your own at home after consulting the textbooks. This is time consuming, but rewarding. One has to be creative while preparing detailed notes and your creativity comes to the fore if you do this. These notes will in turn become a permanent asset for you.

CHAPTER 37

Choice of Vocation

It is very important to choose the right vocation, the one that suits you best. A person's potential can be fully utilized only if he is in the right profession. Your appetite will not be satisfied unless you get the food of your choice. For full satisfaction you must eat that which you like. Similarly, to perform well, you have to choose the job you will enjoy doing. J. Krishnamurti has said: "Happiness comes when you are doing something because you really love to do it, and not because it gives you riches or makes you a prominent figure." One should listen to one's inner voice in choosing the profession, and there will not be any place for vacillation. The decision itself will ensure a comfortable future, and soon success will be yours.

This of course doesn't mean that you need not put any effort. A true vocation is like a hobby that you pursue for the love of it. What makes Maradona a great footballer, Tendulkar a brilliant cricketer, and Rabindranath Tagore a great poet? These people became successful because they are absolutely suited for their vocations.

Some students get carried away by the fame of a particular institute and insist that they would only study there, even though they do not get admission to the branch they want to pursue. There was a girl who was obsessed with IIT Kharagpur. As her score wasn't high enough in the entrance Test (IIT JEE), she did not get admission to the course of her choice, Electronics, at IIT Kharagpur. But in other colleges she would have got a seat for Electronics. Ignoring all well-wishers' advice she joined the course of Architecture at IIT Kharagpur. As a result, she failed miserably in her profession and ended up as a housewife.

Often certain courses and careers are thrust upon the children by their parents and relatives. Children become the victims of their parents' whims. Selecting the true vocation is the 'stepping stone', and going for the wrong vocation against your aptitude is the 'stopping stone'.

CHAPTER 38

A Timetable for Study

Long hours of study without focus or organization doesn't really help. There are students who spend a long time studying, but there won't be anything extraordinary about their results. This is because their method is wrong. Systematic study is essential for success. Hard work and consistency are key to success in an examination. A busy man may get eroded by work pressure, and a lazy man gets corroded by lethargy. Though both are bad, erosion is preferred to corrosion. If you want some work done, give it to a busy man and never to a lazy man. There can be two schedules of study: one for the examination time and the other for the rest of the term. I have given below a sample study timetable for examination time. It can be followed during the preparation leave.

Timetable

7.00 – 8.00	Morning Chores
8.00 – 11.00	Study
11.00 – 11.30	Tea-break
11.30 – 1.00	Study
1.00 – 2.00	Lunch-break
2.00 – 5.00	Study
5.00 – 6.00	Tea-break
6.00 – 9.00	Study
9.00 – 10.00	Dinner
10.00 – 11.30	Study
11.30 – 7.00	Sleep

Nothing will prevent a student from succeeding if he rigorously follows a timetable of the above kind. You may study for twelve hours one day. But you find it hard to give six hours every day for a fortnight. Consistency and adherence to routine are important but difficult too. Once you try to follow a timetable, you will know how hard it is. But you will also soon realize how effective it is.

CHAPTER 39

Be Aware of the Subject, Don't Beware of It

Are you frightened by the boards some people display at their gates: 'Beware of Dogs'? Some students are frightened in the same way by their subjects. Also some teachers and seniors intensify it by making a spectre of difficult subjects. They inject fear in the minds of students by projecting certain subjects as hard. At the most they may pass, with a poor score. A comparatively hard subject is to be tackled with the right attitude. Even if you find a subject unnerving, try to enter it and understand it. Continuous effort will make it easy for you.

You should train your mind to face challenges and difficult circumstances. Always remember that however hard an examination may be, there is a section of students who pass it in the very first attempt and with good marks. They have no magical power. Their plus points are hard work, proper method and a clear understanding of the subjects.

Have a fearless mind that will accept the subject as a reality and then face it. Accepting the problem and the readiness to deal with it mean solving half of the problem.

CHAPTER 40

Do Not Label Subjects As Easy and Difficult

There is a very common trend among the students to separate the subjects into two groups. One group contains comparatively easy subjects. Those subjects are mostly theoretical and can be managed even without any teaching and just by mugging up. The other group contains the hard subjects. Sometimes the students don't read the difficult subjects at all. Some students are so scared of these subjects that in the first attempt they don't even appear for the examination. Is it not a foolish approach? From the dawn of human civilization procrastination of an issue has always made matters more complicated. The first chance is the golden chance. When the student has to pass the particular subject, why should he postpone it? If any student appears for any examination without any preparation, he is bound to fail. Examination is not about taking chances or gambling. The reasons for failure are i) Fear ii) Lack of a clear concept iii) Lack of practice and iv) Negative attitude.

A negative-minded student always strives for only the passing marks, and rarely does he achieve his aim. Don't fail mentally before the actual failure takes place. I remember a strong-willed relative of mine who had cancer, and he was admitted into the hospital. Friends, relatives and well-wishers were continuously consoling him. Suddenly he told me to tell them that cancer cannot kill him, because cancer is only a disease. He jokingly said, "I would not die of cancer." Really it happened. He suffered from fourth stage cancer nearly for five years, but ultimately he died of a heart attack. This example should give some hope to fear-stricken minds that are already defeated even before facing the problem. If you eat only very delicious food, and stop eating essential nutritious items, your health will suffer. In fact most of the tempting foods are harmful to health. Similarly, if you go on reading only easy subjects, you will not get comprehensive knowledge. Select at least one hard subject and have mastery over it. Do things that common people can't.

CHAPTER 41

Make Your Work Your Play

During my school days I had a particular slot for chemistry in my study schedule. I had pasted this schedule on the damp wall of our drawing room. One day a friend of my elder brother visited us and appreciated my systematic nature. He gave me a priceless piece of advice: "Never count hours while reading any hard subject; just read it as a story book. If you feel tired, keep a bookmark and go to the football ground." This is one of the best pieces of advice I have got. If we can find recreation in our work, work becomes enjoyment. You cannot work for a longer time if you don't enjoy it. When you are doing a thing of your liking, you will not feel tired. Tiredness is a state of mind. After half an hour of reading a textbook you feel tired, but you are totally gripped by a thriller for an entire day. What I want to emphasize is the power of complete involvement. You cannot start to make your work your play overnight, but continuous devotion will achieve this too.

CHAPTER 42

Be Sincere, but Don't Be Serious

> "Seriousness is nothing but sadness; it is another name of sadness."
>
> —Osho

Serious people rarely laugh. A person who rarely laughs rarely enjoys his life. Love and laughter are the two integral components of happiness. If you keep distance from one out of the two, the chance of being happy is reduced by fifty per cent.

Generally, we want a flying start. When a newcomer joins a gym, he wants to lift the heaviest weights and do the hardest exercises. But the coach doesn't allow that. All of us want maximum success overnight with minimum effort.

Many natural phenomena give us lessons for life. For example, a river originates on a mountain as a small stream. On the way it grows and becomes a mighty river. A humble beginning can lead to a glorious future. Many of the business tycoons have started their careers with only a few shillings. A big tree sprouts from a little seed.

If you are sincere about your work, the result will automatically follow. Never become too serious. Serious people are generally unhappy. Unhappiness leads to cynicism. Nobody likes a cynical person. Sincerity alone is enough for a happy life. If someone fails despite sincerity, it is bad luck. But experience tells us that luck accompanies the toiling hands.

CHAPTER 43

Importance of Good Results

> "Quality is never an accident, it is always the resultant of an intelligent effort."
>
> —John Ruskin

To survive in a highly competitive environment, you must have good examination results. Ideally, you should score high in all papers. Here the term 'good result' is used in a relative sense. The minimum requirement is a first class. If you can score enough to win a distinction, it is definitely praiseworthy.

Gaining knowledge is no doubt more important than scoring high. The knowledge will always stand us in good stead. But the world wants to see proof on paper. And in competition an impressive mark sheet counts. It is never just to measure knowledge by the examination score. Nevertheless your score will be what decides your career. If your record isn't good, nobody will ever pay serious attention to you. Therefore, a good result is your trump card for an interview or any other selection procedure.

There are many postgraduates who do not know the basics of their subject, and if asked, they admit as much. We mug up the lesson, commit the text to memory and vomit it out in the examination. We decorate our egos with the degrees we have earned and rest on them for ever. A man with a Doctorate will think of a postgraduate as an inferior. The postgraduate in his turn will look down upon a graduate. A degree must not be a means to outsmart others and bolster one's false pride.

CHAPTER 44

Knowledge of English

Knowledge of English may not be something to be proud of, but if you don't know it you are in for a disadvantage. This is a serious problem for students whose medium of education is not English but another language. It is no surprise that even many postgraduates of our country fail to communicate well in English. This is often because of shyness and fear of making mistakes. Learning anything at a later age proves difficult, like swimming and cycling for example. In our country there are two groups of students: one educated through the medium of English, and the second, taught through an Indian language. The second group is often poor in English. While communicating with students of English medium, they suffer from an inferiority complex. They cannot express even things they know well. There are many who cannot write a simple letter in English. They generally tend to avoid the use of English. They try to manage all the odd situations with a passable knowledge. They show their hatred for the English language. The hatred for English is nothing more than a disguise for their feeling of inferiority. In the era of privatization, when there are few government jobs waiting for us, a working knowledge of English is essential.

CHAPTER 45

Don't Worry about the Job Too Early

Some students start thinking about the job right from the day of their admission to college. They are living in a world of fantasy. It is often pressure from the family and the society that makes students unrealistically career-minded. It is ridiculous for a man of twenty-five to think about the pension he will get after retirement. An obsession with security may be the expression of an unconscious fear of insecurity. A general career plan is more than enough. Planning for the future is good, but it should not be at the cost of the present. Do every job at the appropriate time, and if your luck is not bad, you are bound to reap its benefits. Instead of working hard if one spends time brooding over the uncertainties of life, he will make life miserable and futile.

CHAPTER 46

Have Realistic Goals

Students must not be overambitious. That means do not crave for success, new degrees, etc. Students and parents are in a mad rat race for professional degrees, which they want by hook or crook. J. Krishnamurti has said: "What you call happiness is the outcome of getting what you want."

Generally people are always unhappy. The moment one wish is fulfilled, they are disturbed by the next. At the end of the day, they feel dissatisfied with all they have got. There is a difference between ambition and craving. If one chases something without realizing his limitations, despair will be the result. We have to be realistic in this respect. If we can strike a balance between our mental world and the material world, we can be considerably free of irrational cravings. The desire to get rich and lack of good education leads us to think irrationally. We begin to reach for the stars and end up ruined. We must pay heed to this advice of David Frost: "Don't aim for success. If you want it, just do what you love and believe in, and it will come naturally." If we strive hard instead of dreaming, we realize that the possibilities are endless. All monomanias lead to unhappiness.

CHAPTER 47

Rapport between Students, Teachers and Parents

> "A total development of the child can be brought about only when there is the right relation between the teachers, students and parents."
>
> — J. Krishnamurti

A good teacher is like a powerful current of fresh air. A good teacher can be compared to a great leader who inspires his followers with the confidence in themselves. Three factors are to be considered for the proper growth of a student. They are love, positive outlook and knowledge. In this age of rat race there is hardly any coordination between the parents and the teachers. In the busy city life all the parents expect good results from their children but how often do they counsel their children? Do they peep into their inner beings? Most of the parents are very happy if the child brings a good score card. Is it enough? Nowadays every person is the victim of diversions and materialistic pleasure. In today's world if you want to see a devoted teacher in a country like India, you will probably have to peep into an ordinary village school rather than a city school. I know a poor lady who is a primary school teacher at Kamshet. Kamshet is a place nearly fifty kilometres from Pune city located in the western part of India. She is employed in a government-aided school. In my whole life I haven't seen any teacher more devoted than her. Due to her poverty she takes private tuitions. Even on holidays and Sundays she teaches for 2–3 hours at a stretch. The fee she charges is so nominal that it may appear ridiculous.

After coaching a child for the whole month (six days per week) she takes Rs 150/- only. It is approximately $3. Can you just think of quality education at such a cheap rate anywhere in the world?

A true teacher is the source of knowledge. A good teacher can be compared to a candle. A small candle is much more powerful than all the darkness of this universe. It is the initial energy, which motivates you. A student may forget his college professors, but rarely does he forget the teachers of his primary school. Primary-school teachers build the foundation of a child's career. However great you may be, you are always very small in front of your teachers. In any city school the day of publication of the result is observed as an open day. Most of the parents go with many grievances. Every parent thinks his child is very intelligent. In this world very few parents accept the lack of efforts put in by their children. Probably no teacher accepts his responsibility for the poor result of his students. Every teacher thinks his teaching is extraordinary and he is the best among his colleagues. Instead of having a proper dialogue with the teacher, guardians start quarrelling, and the little child becomes the victim of that negative atmosphere. Negative atmosphere injects negativity. Nowadays education has become a good business without any risk. A teacher must not be quarrelsome, but should have a positive and pleasant personality.

Students must remember that education is not just a means to a degree and a job. To gain knowledge you should be devoted. No pains, no gains. Do you think only the students are responsible for this state of affairs? Definitely not. If there had been proper counselling from the childhood, their mental set-up would have been different. Every parent gives advices to the child. But before preaching they must practise what they preach.

CHAPTER 48

Time Management

"Yesterday is a cancelled cheque, tomorrow is a promissory note, and today is the ready cash. Use it."

—Anonymous

He is intelligent who knows how to use time. Worthy use of time is an art. Everybody gets twenty-four hours per day. How he spends it differs from person to person. Right from my childhood I have often heard a common saying, "Don't waste time." Do you think you can waste time? How can you waste time? You can waste something that belongs to you. You can waste money if you have it. But no one possesses time, so time can't be wasted; it can only be used. Using your time in an optimized way is time management. For the proper growth of a successful career, time management is essential.

I want to give a simple example. Generally in any big city if you go to a doctor (even with an appointment), you have to wait for 1 to 1½ hour. Whenever I visit any doctor, I observe the impatient patients. These patients are the victims of boredom. Again and again they look at their watches, and their facial expressions become rigid. Instead of doing that, if anyone just carries a book with him, he can use his time productively. When his turn comes, he can go to the doctor for consultation. If anyone doesn't know time management, he is bound to fail in his profession. Once I visited a patient (he was my distant relative) in a famous city hospital. He was a rich but inactive fellow. His age was around seventy, and throughout his life he didn't do any creative thing. He only enjoyed his ancestral properties, but he spent the stored wealth very practically in a calculated way. When I visited him, he was taking rest. When I gently knocked at the door, he opened his eyes and started sobbing. He had become very emotional. I still remember one sentence he said. He said, "Today at the end of my life I have realized how small the life is. In my next birth I will do work right from my childhood. I have simply wasted my life." What he had said was an absolute truth. If a person wastes his life and realizes the value of time in the twilight of his life, then nothing can be done. You can reverse everything except the hands of a clock. One very important aspect of time management is to use the available time in the proper sequence. Postponement is one of the dangerous games that human beings play to gain more time. So right now if you promise to use time properly, your life can take a good turn. One must avoid gossiping. Write off your past and have a look to your present and future. Success is bound to come if proper time management is achieved. Either you have to manage the time or the time will manage you. Start managing the time right from this moment. The golden sunrise of tomorrow is waiting with success in store.

CHAPTER 49

Guidelines to Take a Written Test

Many students score less because of avoidable mistakes. But if you keep in mind a few basic things, you will not commit these mistakes. Here is a list of guidelines that will help you score more in a written test.

i) Give margins on both sides of your answer sheet in all the papers and number the pages.
ii) Always start with a simple theoretical question. If you start with a mathematical problem and feel that it is wrong, you cancel it and the initial presentation gets spoilt. So you must start with a simple theoretical question for having a good start.
iii) Your handwriting may become relatively bad at the end hours as you rush in order to complete the paper, but if it is good in the first few pages, it draws the attention of the examiner. So the handwriting in the first few pages must be good.
iv) Draw the figures wherever required and label them properly. Never use red pen or red pencil. Draw the figures in such a way that it will be equidistant from both the margins.
v) Use your own calculator, drawing instruments and pens. They must be in extremely good condition.
vi) If you take supplementary answer sheet, write your examination seat number properly on it and follow the page numbering in continuation with the main answer sheet. If you take more than one supplement, do the proper numbering in the successive supplements.

vii) Show the rough calculations on the last page of the main answer sheet and scratch it by double line in a crisscross way at the end of the examination.

viii) Distribute the time in such a way that at the end of the examination at least you get fifteen minutes for checking the answers.

ix) Whenever you solve a mathematical problem, check it immediately twice. Enough time is not available at the end. Never wait for the last minutes. At the end of the examination you are supposed to check only the overall write-up, not the mathematical mistakes. Because at the end even if you find a mistake you will not be in a position to rectify it due to the shortage of time.

x) If you are a student of science, be very particular about the unit conversion. Convert all the units to SI system.

xi) Whenever you solve a mathematical problem, give all the steps properly, number all the equations properly and at the end block the final answer by a rectangle.

xii) Whenever any short note is to be written, don't write irrelevant things. Give the necessary drawings wherever required. Give the required mathematical equations. One equation is much more powerful than ten lines of explanation. Be brief and give the answers to the point.

xiii) Sometimes you may get some superfluous data in your question. You must have the adequate preparation to ignore them; otherwise you will be confused.

xiv) Attempt all the questions and try to answer them properly. Try to give the maximum output.

If you follow these points, you are bound to get a better result.

CHAPTER 50

How to Give Oral Examination

There is no unique method for giving oral examination. It depends on the examiner. Students must not be nervous before the oral examination. Till date I have conducted the oral examination of nearly eight thousand students, and most of the time I've found the students totally unprepared for it. Even the most talkative student becomes tongue-tied. Students don't reply to a single question and their silence irritates the examiners. Initially the examiner asks the basic questions, and when a good candidate gives correct answers one after the other the examiner tries to fluster the candidate by asking some tricky questions. This is nothing but the examiner's ego, but that is not at all damaging for the candidate. Very few examiners of the world want the candidate to answer all the questions.

Once during an oral examination another examiner and I were examining a very brilliant girl. The co-examiner was a retired professor of a famous engineering college. The girl was giving correct answers to all the questions, and my co-examiner also went on shooting a volley of questions. Lastly when the girl failed to answer one very difficult question, I observed a brittle smile on the face of that old teacher, and the girl was allowed to go. I was giving marks. The score was taken out of fifty marks. I was entering the marks on a rough page, and it was to be entered in the final mark sheet at the end of the exam. I gave her 40. Suddenly my co-examiner snatched the pen gently from my hand and changed the 0 to 8 and 40 was changed to 48. I was really surprised. What a human touch and judgement! This is the essence of an oral examination. Good candidates get proper justice. The students have to overcome the in-built fear and prepare well. Secondly, the student must have a smart and decent look before appearing for any oral examination.

CHAPTER 51

Be Computer Savvy

In today's world basic knowledge of the computer is essential. You are not supposed to have advanced knowledge of computing, but at the same time you must not have computer-phobia. Many people (especially the old generation) show no interest at all in acquiring computer knowledge because of their in-built fear of the computer. Everyone must accept the changed technology. It is difficult, but according to Karl Marx, "Change is inevitable". If we don't accept the change, we will perish. If any person is not an engineer or a computer professional, he is not supposed to know the computer languages or programming. But he must have the basic knowledge of computer and the rudimentary knowledge of the Internet. The power of the Internet is unbelievable. Just imagine that you can compose a draft and send it to 30–40 people across the globe at a time just by a single click of a mouse. It will definitely reach the proper hands, and if the email ID is wrong, the mail will bounce back. Secondly, 100% privacy is maintained with the secret password. What more do you expect? Just imagine the traditional method. In earlier days a letter used to take 10–20 days to reach America from India and there was no guarantee about the delivery of the letter. Email is the greatest boon of the modern technology. Apart from that there are several other facilities. You need not collect volumes of *Encyclopaedia Britannica* in your personal library; you may have ready access to it through the web. The Internet has proved that the world is a small place, because your views and thoughts can reach a remote village of Africa or the snow-laden Alaska within a fraction of a second. We must update ourselves. Sharpening of knowledge at regular intervals is necessary. Elbert Hubbard has said, "It is a fine thing to have ability, but to discover ability in others is the true test." People have ability. They only require a spark from outside. That will motivate them. Once I helped an eighty-year-old man to compose an email and send it. I made a suitable mail ID for that old man. His mail ID is *modern_octogenarian@hotmail.com*

That old man initially resisted, but nowadays when I visit his house, I invariably find him browsing the sites related to fine arts and painting. The glint in his old pair of eyes expresses his gratitude. Still there are many young men who don't have their mail IDs. I say jokingly, "It doesn't matter if you don't have your own identity, but your mail ID is essential for the survival in this age of communication."

I have visited I.I.T. Powai and I.I.M. Kolkata. They are educational institutes which produce researchers, engineers and managers of very high calibre. The most beautiful thing that I observed in those institutes was the students' computer awareness. I witnessed students working whole night in the computer centre. Computer-knowledge is very helpful for synthesising thoughts. It matters a lot whether you possess the rudimentary knowledge of the Internet or not. If the answer is positive, sharpen your knowledge; and if it is negative, create your mail ID right now and go ahead. In our childhood we are scared while riding a cycle, but once we learn to balance, it becomes difficult for us to separate ourselves from the cycle. Same is the case with computer. Learning anything new may create initial fear or trauma, but we soon overcome it as we get the hang of it.

CHAPTER 52

GRE and TOEFL

These are the two examinations which have gained a steady popularity since 1975, and now these two names are very common. There is hardly a student who doesn't know about them. It is essential to pass these two examinations for pursuing higher studies in USA. Thousands of students go to USA every year from different countries like India, China, Bangladesh and Philippines. Apart from these there are many other countries also. But the major chunk of students come from Asia, because Asia is the most densely populated continent. Once a politician jokingly said, "Wipe out Asia from the globe, most of the problems will be solved." Definitely from the population point of view he might be justified, but these Asians have major roles in developed countries like USA and UK. A major cross-section of NASA consists of Indians.

GRE means Graduate Record Examination and TOEFL means Test of English as a Foreign Language. There are very few students who get low score in TOEFL. One must score 213 out of 300 in TOEFL. But the students from the vernacular medium face difficulty in TOEFL. For scoring well in this exam, it is essential that one is very familiar with the American accent. There are audio aids which help the students. But in GRE the score matters a lot. Out of 1600 if you get 1300 or more, you are on the safer side. Though it depends on the stream. In earlier days there used to be GRE examination on paper, and there used to be particular dates. Till 2004 the total score of GRE was 2400. Nowadays the pattern is absolutely student-friendly. The exam is to be given online, and you can appear on any day according to your convenience. Only you have to take the date from the examination authority. You may not have to be a graduate. One can appear for GRE exam in the pre-final year or final year of his undergraduate studies. Earlier there used to be three sections in GRE. One was language and vocabulary, the second one was basic mathematics and aptitudes related to rudimentary mathematics, and the last one was test of logic or test of reasoning. Since the second part was related to school-level mathematics, it was the easiest part of the whole exam. Nowadays there are only two sections each of 800 marks. They are English and aptitude. Apart from these there is essay writing. For that the marks obtained are not counted. But one must get 3.5 points out of 6.0 points in essay writing. For an exam like GRE a candidate need not have great imagination or very high intelligence. The required qualities are speed and accuracy. Any American university considers four factors before giving admission to a student. They are given below according to the descending order of importance. Though this order may vary from university to university. The general order is

i) GRE score
ii) Overall academic progress
iii) Recommendation (generally three recommendations are required)
iv) SOP, i.e., Statement of Purpose.

Assuming that the candidates who appear for GRE possess an above-average academic track record, I would like to give stress only on GRE score. Good GRE score requires good and regular practice. Go on giving dummy examinations as often as possible. Don't do a half-hearted preparation. For appearing in any examination, whether it is GRE or any other exam, you must do thorough preparation. You must try to get good results in the first chance. In my teaching career I have recommended innumerable students to various American universities and other universities across the globe. From my experience I can say: most of the students get a standard GRE score, which is neither bad nor very good. So you must try to have a very good GRE score. By your score itself you can eliminate others. To get admission is not a very difficult thing, but if your score is low, you have to compromise with the choice of your university and you may have to even compromise with the branch of study for which you opt. Lastly with a low score in this age of cut-throat competition, you can't think of financial aid. So when the score is so important, adequate labour and time must be given. Sometimes it becomes really difficult to prepare simultaneously for GRE and your subject of graduation (it may be engineering, science, arts or commerce). I have found many good students appearing for GRE after completion of their graduation. Obviously they lose one year. They pursue their MS after a gap of one year. But during that gap they mainly prepare for GRE, and sometimes they take up a job. It is up to you, which way you choose.

CHAPTER 53

Effects of Practical Training

> "It is good to have enthusiasm. It is good to have will, but it is essential to have training."
>
> —Jawaharlal Nehru

How true the above saying is! It becomes more true when the training is a practical one. It may be cooking or surgery. In our country there is an ever-widening gulf between the theoretical examination system and the practical application of learning. Students solve fourth order differential equations, partial heterogeneous differential equations and pass the examinations. But if you ask them the physical significance of a differential equation, they falter, because they don't know it. Always the academic activities are at low ebb because of the lack of practical training. Unless the gulf between the theory and the practical is bridged, we can't go ahead with a good speed. To have thorough practical knowledge there is only one method. One has to involve himself continuously in practical training. There is a famous Chinese proverb: "Tell me and I will forget; show me and I may remember, involve me and I will understand."

You will surely appreciate the essence of this proverb. Nothing is more important than involvement. There must be totality in involvement. If you belong to a team of mechanical engineers in an engine room of a ship, never try to keep distance from the machines. Touch it, feel it, love it, repair it and get totally blackened by the oil and grease of the engine. That machine oil is the true ornament for an engineer. Unless you get yourself blackened, you can't really understand the working of the machine. In a partially cold atmosphere for taking bath if you continuously think of hot water, you can't enjoy the winter. For enjoying the winter, you must pour cold water over your body at least once. That is essential.

There is a joke about how 'theoretical' people can be. While on a visit to a wildlife sanctuary, a group of students, along with the professor, was suddenly attacked by a lion. The professor advised the students to keep calm. He told the boys, "Have you not read my book about lions, in which I have mentioned that if one stares at a lion and keeps calm, it will not be harmful." One student replied, "But has the lion read your book?" This joke makes clear how theory and practice are miles apart. If proper steps are not taken, the gulf will be wider. I have met many doctors who don't know how to push injection in a comparatively less painful way. This is due to lack of practice. They are not familiar with the pushing angle. If you ask them, their ego gets hurt. Immediately they say, "To push the injection is the job of a nurse, it is not a doctor's job." They can't shrug off their responsibility by giving such a reply. They are not supposed to do the job of a nurse. I do agree with them. But there is a question. Are they doing their own job properly? Once one Bengali went to England and stayed there for five years. After returning to Bengal he announced that he had completely forgotten Bengali. Then an eminent person gave a very humorous comment. He said, "It is sad that you have forgotten Bengali, but it is sadder that you couldn't learn English well in the last five years." This comment is totally applicable to most of the doctors of today's world. Neither do they know nursing nor diagnosis. There is a famous quotation about doctors. It is given below.

> "A touch that never hurts;
> A temper that never tires;
> A heart that never hardens."
>
> —Dr. Lucis

To how many doctors is this quotation applicable?

Probably very few doctors qualify for such a compliment in this money-making age. Everybody knows his shortcomings, but tries to hide it behind the curtain of his puffed-up ego. Whether a man is a student or teacher, the cause of his ego is his faults. In this world no one will come forward to teach us. It is we who have to take the initiative. If you are a student of mechanical engineering, just go to the nearby garage and get yourself thoroughly trained. With your strong theoretical background of Engineering be a garage boy who knows the differential equations and its applications. It is priceless. If you really do that, you will be the best mechanical engineer in the world.

CHAPTER 54

Role of Good Recommendation

Good recommendation from one's professor is important, and it becomes crucial when one wants to pursue a career at an international level. I have recommended many students for various universities located in different continents of the globe. I have found that even a non-deserving candidate wants strong recommendation. There are several parameters which are to be considered while recommending a student. His motivation, honesty, written expression, verbal expression, teaching capability, research potential, integrity, emotional stability and many other things are to be considered while recommending a student. There are rating charts. In the forms of some universities they give grades, e.g. poor, average, good, very good and excellent.

The overall assessment of the candidate by his/her recommender is of utmost importance. It is of no use to recommend a candidate with reservation. I suggest that the teaching community should either recommend a student without reservation or not to recommend him at all. It is useless to recommend a candidate with reservation. It damages the candidate's career and throughout life the candidate becomes unhappy with the concerned recommender. Students also know whom to approach for getting the recommendation. They always prefer to approach an approachable junior professor rather than a cynical and sceptical senior professor. Good recommendation may not be able to do too much of good, but a slightly bad recommendation can cause a lot of harm. So one should be doubly careful before choosing his recommender. Some students go by the status of his professor. They think if they get the recommendation from their HOD or Principal, it will add some extra weightage in their admission process. It is absolutely wrong. The most important thing is whether your recommender has personally taught you or not. The recommender mainly gives his personal view about the student. As a recommender your project guide can play a better role than your HOD or Principal. Secondly, recommendation comes at the end. Before approaching for getting recommended one must give his bio-data to his recommender so that he can know about the other activities and extra curricular activities of the candidate. It is observed that while trying to get a recommendation, the students meet professors hundred times, and we the teachers rate them very high. After the purpose is served, they turn away and forget their professors totally. They leave all the connections behind. It is definitely not good on the part of the students. But after all they are our students. We don't hold it against them. It is they who are requested to think over this matter.

CHAPTER 55

Value of Teaching Habit

"To teach is to learn twice."

—Japanese proverb

Students should teach also. There is an age-old proverb, "Teaching is the best learning aid in the world." When I was in 8th standard there was a boy in my class named Joseph. He was senior to me by age. He had failed in the same class twice. I have always felt quite comfortable with others. Gradually that boy and I became close to each other. My family members, teachers and well-wishers didn't like it. I was a relatively good student, so everybody thought that if I continued to be friendly with that boy, his evil influence would degrade me. I laughed it away and started teaching him the same mathematics and science which I was simultaneously learning with him in the class. In the class he used to keep calm and rarely did he follow what the teachers taught. But when I taught him, he began to understand things. I used to cross-check whether he had really understood or not. Since there was not much gap in our age, he became very frank with me. Gradually Joseph improved, and in the secondary examination he secured more marks in Biology than I. It really made me happy, though others didn't like it. Teaching means spreading of knowledge and information. One can only teach well if he comes down to the student's level. His faculties of observation must be very keen. He must be able to judge their mind. Very rarely do the students admit that they don't understand. From their body language and from their eyes the teacher has to judge. A man with too systematic and theoretical attitude can be a clerk but can't be a teacher. I would like to share a joke.

Colleague: Ah! Professor, I heard your daughter has had twins. Boys or girls?

Professor: Well one is a girl and the other is a boy. But vice-versa is true.

This type of a professor who keeps records should be a record-keeper. Teaching is an art. Seldom do we find a teacher who can teach how to teach. The art of teaching is an experience, which can only be felt. It is just a form of energy that comes from within.

CHAPTER 56

Participate in Different Programmes

In my life I have attended many programmes. I have attended various seminars, workshops and conferences. In one conference I was listening to the speech of an eminent person. He spoke for nearly forty-five minutes. Only one of his sentences got ingrained in my mind. He said, "This conference may prove itself useless for me, but whatever I am today is due to the hundreds of conferences and programmes that I attended." How true his comment is! You can realize it. If you go on attending different conferences gradually your periphery of knowledge will increase. You get bigger exposure, and there you can project your ideas and exchange your views and thoughts with a wider cross-section of people. You may think you are the greatest if you stay alone, but if you start mixing with people, you will feel you are one of those great people. Wherever there is public relation, involve yourself. Let it be the committee of the college magazine or a cricket match between Principal's eleven and Students' eleven. Participation brings ecstasy and exchange of views and thoughts gives you the platform to unfurl your views and ideas in front of other experts. Definitely a student of first year is not supposed to attend many conferences and seminars, but from pre-final year one should start attending seminars and conferences. It allows you to know new people and you can keep a very happy frame of mind. For any conference the inauguration function and valedictory function are the two integral parts. A conference can be called the miniature replica of our life. It starts, it grows and it ends. To understand life in a better way you have to understand yourself; and for knowing yourself, you have to understand others. There are several types of conferences and seminars on different subjects. Attend those which you like. Let us assume that you didn't attend any conference till date. Take the due initiative to attend one conference, then gradually attend ten, and see the difference. The difference itself will be the experience. By attending conferences you will only gain something. There is nothing to lose.

CHAPTER 57

Group Discussion

Group discussion is most commonly known as GD. Nowadays it is one of the major stages of any selection procedure. It is another name of elimination. In any group discussion, a group of candidates are allowed to sit together. One topic is given to them and then starts the brainstorming session. In my institute I was the staff advisor from the Civil Engineering Department for the training and placement cell for a couple of years. I personally experienced many group discussions. There was less of discussion and more of shouting. Those who shout louder are those who dominate. Particularly a student who doesn't have the fluency in English feels like a fish out of water in a GD. Most of the times the boys and the girls talk in an irrelevant way, but the speed and gift of the gab are counted. Your arguing and fighting capacity with a coating of diplomacy is mainly measured in a GD. In any GD never think that the others are inferior or superior to you, just think you are one of them. Nobody can excel in GD overnight. Continuous practice is required. Education is not only book-based. The famous philosopher J. Krishnamurti defined education in the following way.

"What is education? It is essentially the art of learning not only from the books, but also from the whole movement of life."

Your friend who excels in the GD can't be superior to you. The main problem is that once we accept any person as superior to us we don't dare to face him. We surrender to him. We must not do that. In this world nobody is superior or inferior. These two terms are relative. By the dint of hard work, determination, perseverance and strong ambition even a patient of polio can be a winner in the Olympics. There are records in the history to prove it. If a polio patient can win gold medal in the Olympics, can't you get through a GD? I state with authenticity, "Yes, you can, you can score more." Only your inner soul needs to be awakened. Continuous defeat and comparison kill 90% of the strength of your inner being. Ignore the previous defeat and criticism. It is the job of the cynics. Promise today; start today, if you don't find anybody, stand in front of a mirror, and talk to yourself. Fix a topic. If it is difficult to speak good English fluently, start abusing. Try to abuse fluently. Let the start be with abusing. It is not so easy to abuse fluently in a language with which you are not very familiar. To quarrel in a language requires total command over it. Start abusing; practise regularly. You must win. The day is not very far which will not be a day full of abuses. It will be a day full of amusement. Because that day you will have attained complete fluency in English. Initially there will be a lot of mistakes. Let it be wrong. No one is correct initially. Don't stop practising. Go ahead with a positive mind. Success is inevitable, and it is yours.

CHAPTER 58

Why Study after Examination

The name of this chapter may seem funny, but there is a hidden meaning within that. Before the examination, students read for even twelve hours per day, but after the examination they refuse to read for even twelve minutes. The students are totally detached from their studies during the holidays between two semesters. This is the reason why nowadays students are learning quickly and forgetting it more quickly. Today's education can be compared to the deletion of a word file by another word file of the same name in Microsoft Word. Have you ever tried to study after the examination? Please do that at least once. You will really enjoy it, because it will be a study not for examination. If you work with a target, you will be stressed, but any work without a target can be enjoyed with a relaxed mood. You can do it in a relaxed way. After the examination if any candidate just gives one-hour time per day during vacation, he can proceed miles ahead. This is the very practical approach to life which will reinforce your learning.

CHAPTER 59

Examination Fever

The reason for examination fever is not only the phobia for the examination. In most of the houses the child becomes the victim of comparison. I was always compared with my elder brother, and it irritated me throughout my childhood. This comparison makes students scared of the examination. Comparison injects pessimistic attitude and nervousness within a child's mind. Psychiatrists can help a child to overcome it, but the guardian's psychology also needs to be changed simultaneously in order to help the child.

One should never think of passing alone. But one must have a higher aim. What can be the worst possible outcome of an examination? One may fail. It must be taken in one's stride. Failure in the examination can be pardoned, but if the mental equilibrium itself is disturbed, that becomes dangerous. One should learn to relax before the examination. Examination is a battle of nerves and that is the reason why one needs to be relaxed. One must not get himself drenched in the drizzle of criticism, but have an umbrella of willpower and confidence to keep it away.

CHAPTER 60

How to Use the Vacation

In the vacation you simply do what your heart desires. In the city life school kids rarely get rest throughout the year. I see school children getting up at 5.00 a.m. and going to bed at 11.00 p.m. because of the pressure of homework. Throughout the year these poor children can't even enjoy a good nap. Nowadays they don't get total freedom even during a vacation. The guardians get their child admitted to the summer camp. The guardians want their children to be jacks-of-all-trades. I remember a funny incident. Once one lady (she was the wife of my colleague) wanted my suggestion regarding sending her son to the summer camp. She wanted me to help her decide if she should or shouldn't send him. Initially I kept mum and then I jokingly advised her to admit her child to a sleeping camp instead of summer camp, where he can regularly enjoy a comfortable sleep for ten hours. Initially she couldn't get me. After a couple of seconds when she realized the irony hidden behind my remark she became upset. My view is that in the vacation you must enjoy adequate sleep and lots of food. Only one-hour time per day may be allotted for recapitulation of the subjects lest they should be erased totally from the mind.

CHAPTER 61

How to Present a Seminar

A very good cake may have a very bad appearance; while on the other hand, a very bad cake may have a very beautiful appearance. This difference is nothing but the way of presentation. Presentation is an art. Seminar is an integral part of undergraduate and postgraduate studies. You mainly require two things for presenting a seminar in a perfect way. The first one is clarity of thoughts related to the topic of the seminar and the second one is enriched English coupled with finest communication skill. Standard of seminar varies from UG level to PG level. Your faculties of thinking must work simultaneously while presenting a seminar. You must be well dressed. In earlier days students used to prepare transparencies for using them in OHP (over head projector). Nowadays with the computer, OHP is considered as an obsolete thing and the new generation prefers PowerPoint presentation. It is easy to handle and less time-consuming. Only the numbers of slides to be prepared are to be planned properly.

CHAPTER 62

How to Tackle the Research Work

Truly speaking, there is no research work in undergraduate classes. There is a dissertation (it is generally applicable only to professional courses) at the end of the curricula in post graduation. But even this dissertation is not a 100% research work. True research work starts at the doctoral level. Since this book is mainly written for the students of undergraduate and postgraduate courses, I am intentionally not peeping into that area. Still I want to say one thing. If you chase a degree, no research work can be done. True research may take huge time and even after that the outcome may be futile. So before plunging into the ocean of research work one is advised to have a test of patience. Research is not a syllabus-oriented study; there is no limit to it. I personally witnessed boys doing two types of work together. One is dissertation work (it can be called a research work in a miniature form) and the second one is hunting for a job. What a contradiction! For doing true research you should be free from all the bondage and must possess an innovative mind. Teachers do Ph.D. for getting promotion and increments. That type of Ph.D. rarely produces good quality research work.

CHAPTER 63

How to Maintain Relations with Your Seniors

In earlier days, the freshers in any engineering or medical college used to know their seniors through the brutal process of ragging, but nowadays this cruelty is limited because of the steps taken by the higher authority. But ragging has not totally vanished. In every college there is a group of idle, pessimistic, cynical and sadistic seniors. They are very poisonous. They give all the wrong ideas and wrong ways to the newly admitted freshers. They inject fear and enjoy doing it. Somehow you have to locate them and avoid them diplomatically. You must have a good liaison and amiable relation with your seniors, but you should never be the victim of their evil influences. I do remember when I entered the Regional Engineering College, Durgapur (presently it is known as NIT, Durgapur) in 1982, I was introduced to most of the teachers by a group of seniors. Most of the things they said about the professors were negative. You must stay away from indulging in criticism, but at the same time you must have normal relation with your seniors.

CHAPTER 64

Comparison between Degree and Knowledge

There can't be any comparison between degree and knowledge. Degree is nothing but a certification. If a person compares degree with knowledge, he should be classified as a classical dunce. The great poet Rabindranath Tagore didn't have any university degree, but his works are the compulsory subjects at postgraduate level. As compared to knowledge, degree is unimportant. If you compare knowledge to a long river, degree, at the most, can be compared to a small tributary. Knowledge is the bridge between the object and the subject. If they are not separated the bridge can't exist. But for survival in this world it is all right if one does not have knowledge. However, he must possess a degree. Without a degree it is difficult to survive in this age of cutthroat competition. The stronger the competition, the more the hankering after degrees. Degree is what ordinary people want, knowledge belongs to the higher class, and wisdom is the end of knowledge. A person with wisdom is enlightened; he never goes after any so-called degree. A visiting card with many degrees and memberships is nothing but the reflection of a childish egotistical mind. Father of Open-Channel Hydraulics VEN-TE-CHOW didn't write 'Dr.' in front of his name in his world-famous book entitled *Open-Channel Hydraulics*. A known face needs no painting. In most of the places degrees are either used as ornaments or as weapons to camouflage one's own weak points. As long as a person chases a degree, he remains ignorant. In this world full of cut-throat competition, degrees and marks are used as the two tools to make the elimination process easy in a competition.

Generally if Dr. 'X' is addressed as Mr. 'X', he becomes angry, because these so called doctorates carry less knowledge and more ego. Their minds are filled with false pride. Unless they empty this bin full of meaningless pride, they can't be truly happy. I never came across any of these so-called 'doctors' who can laugh freely. Their degree became their burden.

CHAPTER 65

How to Overcome Shyness

Some students are excessively shy, and they pay for this nature. In the outer world shyness doesn't pay. A student with a shy nature must come out of his shell and many times this student requires thorough counselling. Sometimes it is better to seek the help of a psychiatrist. That age is very vulnerable. A student goes through a transition, which joins boyhood and manhood. A student's mind contains both the simplicity of a boy and complexity of a man. Many times I have found teachers, especially school-teachers, criticizing a boy with shy nature. That is absolutely wrong. There are many students who have many doubts, but they never ask a single question in the class because of their shy nature.

> "To ask a question may bring a moment's shame, but not to ask and remain ignorant is a life-time of shame."
>
> —Anon

A shy student must try to overcome his shyness, otherwise he is bound to suffer in this smart world. They should try again and again and till the end they must continue their effort. Here is another piece of wisdom.

> "Being defeated is often a temporary condition, giving up is what makes it permanent."
>
> — Marilyn Vos Savant

How true it is! You must have heard the story of Robert Bruce, who was inspired by a spider. One must not surrender. Another name of surrender is death of mind. There is no substitute to willpower. Tremendous amounts of talent and energy are present in each human being. Nobody will help you. It is you who has to awaken himself. During the crucifixion, Jesus Christ carried his own cross. If Lord Jesus could help himself, why not we?

CHAPTER 66

Don't Develop a Complex

A man can be either without complex or he will have both the complexes (inferiority and superiority). It is because the so-called complexes can be compared to the two sides of a coin. The term superiority complex is commonly known as ego. One famous philosopher said, "To me ego doesn't carry any meaning. 'E' stands for entry and 'GO' stands for exit. If you possess ego and come to me, then you are free to leave through the exit." Ego is the root cause of 90% problems in the modern society. If inferiority complex dominates within you, you will be the sufferer, and if superiority complex dominates, then others will suffer. If you develop inferiority complex, you allow others to bully you, while if you have a superiority complex, others will suffer due to your high-handed manner. Both are bad. If you have some knowledge you may be proud, that much can be accepted, but the contained pride must not surface itself as ego. Inferiority complex separates you from the rest of the society. So try to be a person free from complexes. If you find it is difficult, then minimize it as much as you can.

CHAPTER 67

Need to Have a Higher Aim

> "The tragedy doesn't lie in not reaching your goal. The tragedy lies in having no goal at all."
>
> —Benjamin Mays

From these words one thing becomes clear, that one must have a goal or aim. Why not have a big aim? We may not be able to scale it, but if we can complete even 50% of a big project, it will be much bigger than any small venture. Generally all the time we attain two-thirds of our aim.

I would like to share a very important personal experience with my readers. It was 1994. One day one of my old students met me with glistening eyes. He had failed seven times in one subject. His father was paralytic, his marriageable sister was till then unmarried, all his subjects of final year were cleared, and only this subject was remaining. The particular paper belonged to the pre-final year. I made a survey and found that all the seven times the boy secured marks which were more than 26 and less than 30. The minimum marks required for passing were 40. All the time he fixed his aim at 40. Two-third of 40 is 26.66. His marks swung between 26 and 30. I gave him a one-line counselling. I told him to fix his aim at 60 because two-third of 60 is 40. He obeyed my advice and cleared the subject in his eighth attempt. This is the benefit of a higher aim. If your aim is low, your thought loses its explosiveness and your creative power becomes partially paralysed. You must have a thought-provoking attitude; otherwise the lack of ambition will not allow the seed of success within your inner being to germinate properly. Your goal or aim must be fixed. Proper goal gives you the right way to go. A proper aim must be coupled with direction, dedication, determination, discipline and deadline.

CHAPTER 68

How to Be Professional

It is extremely difficult to be truly professional, that too for twenty-four hours and three hundred and sixty-five days. Professionalism is a great quality in the outer world. To be truly professional one must be a good actor too. Concession in style, precision in thought and decision in life are the three key elements of professionalism. I would like to share an experience of mine. I experienced it in a private company long back. I went to visit a manager. There was red light outside his cabin. Entry was restricted. The peon requested me to wait. After nearly fifteen minutes one handsome person came and asked the peon slowly, "Has he finished all the biscuits?" Afterwards I came to know that this manager was fond of different varieties of biscuits, and while enjoying biscuits he used to put on the red light outside his cabin for having an undisturbed munching of his favourite brand. Do you think it is professionalism? There is an ambiguity. His staff knew his weak points. For them it was a childish attitude, but for outsiders it was great professionalism. In the professional world you have to prove that you are busy and not very easily approachable. Unless you keep the visitors waiting for a couple of minutes, they don't take you seriously. It is the style of the Indian managers. Most of the times it is found that the secretary of a big shot throws more weight. Definitely it is not professionalism. It is the projection of wickedness. You must not be a person with a light ear, you must be able to judge the psychology of the people and you must not say one's weak point to another. Be friendly, but don't be a friend of everybody around you.

Punctuality is one of the key qualities of a professionally successful person, and two more aspects are a balanced temper and stoic attitude. During success you must not show an over-joyous attitude and during failure you must not behave erratically. If the society knows your mood swings like a pendulum, they will definitely take advantage of your good mood. All the relations are man-made. During examination and illness you are left alone. Then very few people are present by your side. Don't be professional to those friends and persons who stand by your side during your difficult days.

CHAPTER 69

Relation between Marks and Knowledge

Relation between marks and knowledge is very complicated. I have already said that a degree and knowledge are vastly different. It is not right to give a sweeping comment regarding the relation between marks and knowledge. Imagine in an examination there are many candidates. Let us take only three out of them. Let the candidates be 'A', 'B' and 'C'. Let the marks of 'A', 'B' and 'C' be 11, 88 and 89 out of 100. Without any hesitation it can be authentically said that the knowledge of 'A' in that particular subject is practically nil as compared to the knowledge of 'B' and 'C'. But if you ask the question, who is more knowledgeable between 'B' and 'C', I may not be able to answer your question. Due to one extra mark in one paper 'C' is superior to 'B', but it doesn't prove that 'C' has more knowledge than 'B' in the same subject. In examination many times I have found very good students committing silly mistakes because of the pressure. It doesn't mean that the candidate doesn't know the subject. When the marks of two candidates are very close to each other, it becomes simply impossible to compare their knowledge. Here it is assumed that the same examiner has checked both the papers. It is experienced that if five examiners check the same paper, the candidate gets five different marks, and there may be a considerable difference between the lowest and the highest mark. So it is wrong to judge the knowledge level of two candidates by their marks, when their marks are very close. In any competition the candidate with higher marks definitely grabs the good position, but it doesn't prove that he is more knowledgeable to his immediate successor in the merit list. The readers may not agree with me, but I hold my view, because this conclusion is made from hundreds of case studies I conducted in my long teaching career.

CHAPTER 70

How to Control Homesickness

Whenever a student joins an institute far from his home, he is supposed to stay in the hostel. Everyone faces initial difficulties to adjust with the hostel life. During this period all the freshers feel very homesick and repeatedly they pay visits to their homes, and it becomes very dangerous for their academic career. Guardians also don't like this attitude but they become helpless. If the distance between the home and the institute is very long there are fewer visits; but when the distance varies between 100–200 kilometres, then initially they visit their homes every week and often bunk their lectures and practicals. After returning from home they give false excuses. If you add oil to the fire, then the flame will increase. Similarly, visiting home often increases one's feeling of homesickness. There is only one solution to this problem. These freshers have to be united and form a group, and they must know the gravity of the problem. With time, in every case, homesickness reduces. I was in hostel during the span of my graduation. One of my friends, who used to visit his home every week in the first semester of the first year, gradually reduced the frequency of his visits. In the last semester (second semester of the fourth year) he didn't pay a single visit to his home. After passing when everybody had left the hostel, he still stayed on for three days and I was his only company during that small span of time. That is nothing but attachment. Even a prisoner looks at the walls of his cell before vacating it when his term ends. That is called attachment and it is a function of time. My counselling has helped many students to control their feeling of homesickness. After my counselling I observed those students, and I observed the changes that took place within them. There is no generalized solution for this homesickness. Homesickness is not a disease. It is a disorder. If you consider repeated visits to your home a medicine, then the same medicine will be the root cause of aggravation of this disease.

CHAPTER 71

Don't Repress Anything

"Expression is life and repression is suicide."

—Osho

Repression is very negative. There are many students who have suffered throughout their student life due to repression. One must be open-minded, free and frank with his teachers. If one ignores a doubt and represses it, nobody will take care of it. Very few teachers are able to read the glint in the eyes of their students. Never repress anything. Continuous repression of anything is bad not only for your academic career, but also for your health. You got only one life and it is priceless, so why not add some values to it? Only when you give values to your thoughts can you add values to your life. Your thoughts can only be valued when your inner repression is let free. Don't repress anything, come forward, discuss, share your views, share your doubts and be a free man with a light heart and crystal-clear concepts.

CHAPTER 72

Importance of Marks

A student who misses a golden chance just for one mark knows the value of marks. I have already discussed the role of marks and given tips on how to score more. From the title of this book it would seem that the whole book is written about how to study and score more. But it is not the only thing discussed in this book. Emphasis is given to all the important areas of life. Examination is one of them. The famous book of Nirad C. Chaudhuri, *The Autobiography of an Unknown Indian*, is an autobiography and at the same time it is the narration of the ancient and contemporary history. This book will be remembered more for its historical importance. Similarly, this book definitely gives a clear idea about scoring more in an examination, but at the same time it embraces all the aspects of a student's life. I do hope this book will help you to score more in every aspect of your life. All the difficulties which the students come across are discussed in detail. If others can score more, why not you? You too can score more. There have been many promising lives that became mundane because of a low score. Don't be a wilting leaf. Be a leaf which is green and glossy. Only your willpower can make you prominent.

CHAPTER 73

How to Use the Preparation Leave and the Gaps between the Examinations

All the students know the crushing routine which starts from the end of the term and continues up to the end of the examination. The week before the commencement of the examination is very important. Every student, whether sincere or insincere, faces the enormity of the task during the examination. It is an art to use the time available during the preparation leave and gap between the examinations. We have earlier discussed the study routine during the preparation leave, but how to use the gaps between the examinations is not discussed earlier. When there is no gap between two successive examinations, the students wish there was minimum one-day's time between the two successive exams. When there is a gap of one day, they think it would have been better if they had got one more day. The reason is that the students don't prepare throughout the year, and they try to manage everything at the eleventh hour. But if the students get a gap of four days between two examinations, they don't study anything on the first day. Again they become the victims of procrastination. The moment people get ample time, they stop working. That is the common human psychology. One should plan how to study. They should study, and at the same time they should practise it by writing. If it is a mathematical subject, the practice is mandatory. Without knowing driving if anybody sits by the side of the driver, driving seems to be very easy. Is it actually so? Driving means not the operation of clutch, brake, gear and steering; it is the optimized and calculated operation of senses. The physical activities of a driver are nothing but the manifestation of the commands given by the brain. It is the same case with mathematics. If we see anyone doing it, it seems to be very easy; but the moment you start practising it, you face difficulty. So practising is essential in the gap between the two examinations. Continuous practice will reduce the chances of silly mistakes and improve the quality of the answers. That will impress the examiner.

CHAPTER 74

Why the Question Papers of the Last Three Semesters Are Very Important

I always advise my students to solve the question papers of the last three semesters for all the subjects. If anyone does that, he would get 50–60% questions common. Problems are not repeated, but you may get a clear idea about the types of the problems which are generally given in the examination. Usually there will be a panel of examiners who set the questions. As long as a panel is not changed, the pattern of questions doesn't change. Generally, once a panel is formed, it exists for at least one to two years. For the autonomous bodies this panel system is not applicable in general. Solving the question papers of the previous semesters can be compared to a dress rehearsal. However sincere and intelligent a student may be, unless he solves the question papers, his nerves don't get trained to face the examination. It is mandatory to solve the question papers of the last three semesters, and it is desirable to solve the question papers of the last ten semesters. Solving of questions is important, and while solving them you must keep the watch by your side. You must see whether you are able to complete all the answers by the stipulated time or not. If you fail to manage the time, you have to be careful. Only solving the questions can give a professional touch to your preparation.

CHAPTER 75

How to Complete the Whole Syllabus

In the previous chapters in some places I have given special emphasis on completing the syllabus. Students say the examination can be managed even without completing the whole syllabus. Even if a student prepares for 60% of the syllabus thoroughly, he can surely pass. But don't you think it is ridiculous? While having dinner if one keeps away from four to five items also, he can satiate his appetite, but why prefer that? Most of the time students don't even read the difficult chapters. They only study easy chapters in order to pass. A difficult topic in a subject can be compared with very palatable and mouth-watering items in a dinner. Does anyone ever refrain from having the dessert, which is served towards the end of the dinner? Never. Everybody wants to relish it. What is applicable to dinner is also applicable to the syllabus. Is it because a physical and mental exercise is required for completing the syllabus that it is avoided? All of us want to have a good result without making an adequate effort. This is an unethical approach. Till date when I remember my primary school days, I feel traumatized. Unfortunately, I was admitted in the same school where my elder brother had his schooling. The difference between his performance and my performance was very small; it was only the question of direction. He used to occupy the merit list from the top and I used to occupy it from the bottom. What a simple difference! One day I couldn't answer a question a teacher asked. When I was asked to give an explanation, I candidly confessed that I had forgotten to read. That teacher became furious and asked, "You didn't forget to eat. How is it that you forgot to study?" I also replied instantly, "Miss, my body wants food. So how can I forget to take the food? But I never felt the urge to read." The slap which I received as a reply to my candid statement still resounds in my ear and the stinging sensation can't be forgotten easily.

I was talking about completion of the syllabus. As I said earlier, one must give maximum stress to the first chapter of each subject. Once the first chapter becomes clear, it is easier to go ahead with a considerable speed. Completion of syllabus is not a matter of time but that of understanding. Most people confuse the two and think that they have to complete a certain portion of the syllabus within a stipulated period of time. Even the teachers are not an exception. I know one over-systematic teacher teaching the subject of 'Surveying'. He had a plan to complete the whole syllabus in 45 lectures. One day the students were in a festive mood and they bunked his lecture and took a common-off. That teacher said, "I am not going to cover the topic which I was supposed to cover today. Next day I will cover the next topic. If I take today's topic in my next lecture, then my schedule will be disturbed and I will require 46 hours to complete my syllabus." What a theoretical approach! Over-systematic persons are very rarely good thinkers. Truly speaking, many of the greatest fools of the earth are over-systematic. Their discipline is the root cause of the death of their thought. My approach is different; unless the doubts of one chapter become clear, one mustn't switch over to the next chapter. In this world you can be the best teacher to yourself. Give adequate time and complete the whole syllabus of all the subjects. Never try to boost your self-esteem of being time bound at the cost of your students not understanding the subject matter in the period you planned.

CHAPTER 76

Importance of Teamwork

Teamwork has tremendous power. A team with good tuning can multiply the efficiency of a person by many times, and the total output can be unimaginable. We Indians lag in teamwork. In a team everyone must be without ego, and no one should count his contribution. One shouldn't take the stress alone. Big ventures are not possible without a good team. If there is defeat, share it; it will reduce. If there is joy, share it too. It will multiply. Whether it is the design of a bridge, a one-day cricket match or an open-heart surgery, the success or failure depends on the team. In a team the role of the team leader or captain is very important. Life is just like an echo. If the leader motivates his member and doesn't keep any distance with his team members, they can do miracle. On the other hand, because of his ego, if the leader or captain separates himself from the rest of the team, the team is bound to fail. So whenever you have to go with others, you must show good sportsmanship. If you wish, you can achieve so much. The success is not beyond your reach.

CHAPTER 77

Concentration versus Attention

Both the terms 'concentration' and 'attention' seem to be very similar, but in reality they are not so. Attention is one step ahead of concentration. Concentration is most often achieved by whipping the mind, but attention comes from inside. A simple example will make it clear. In the class of a very strict teacher you will find all the students are listening to him. Can it really happen that all the boys and girls are having concentration at a time? Is it not difficult? But if you see a boy looking at a beautiful flower through the window, then without any hesitation you can say that the boy's attention is hundred per cent. With concentration you shrink your mind but with attention you become engrossed. So be attentive. In a dark night if you want to see anything you must focus your torch on the object itself, but if your hand shivers, the beam of light will also move and you will not be able to locate the thing. So be attentive, and have a great going.

CHAPTER 78

Remember, Life Is Not a Journey of a Few Days

Often I find students feeling very frustrated for small reasons. This type of frustration is very perturbing. In one college a student missed distinction by a few marks, and he committed suicide. This is nothing but the manifestation of depression, which was ingrained but not detected by the teachers and the parents. Most of the time the parents and family members laugh at a depressed child and when any mishap takes place, they start crying. Remember one thing, life is not a journey of a few days. Never be saturnine because of failures. Failure is a part of life just like success; only you have to be careful so that the number of failures becomes negligible as compared to the number of successes. Even a great batsman sometimes gets out for a duck. Is it not failure? Should he declare his retirement? Obviously not. Every moment can be the starting point of your career. Never be depressed when you fail. If you fall on the ground, take the help of the same ground and rise again. Who knows, there may be a greater success in disguise behind the failure. While going through a straight road, stop suddenly. Look straight and see as much as you can and fix a point where you have to reach. Start again and head towards the point which is fixed already. Reach the point and stop again and find another target. By this way in a slow but steady method reach your destination. In this way in the journey of life also complete your work schedule step by step. Note that every moment is the starting point and conquer the future in steps accompanied by proper planning, determination and motivation. Never be upset by failures.

Once one oncologist predicted the death of a cancer patient and he told ruthlessly, "Your days are numbered." After a couple of months the oncologist died of an accident but that cancer patient is till date alive with the help of advanced technologies and medicines. This is the colour of life. It changes its path as a river meanders. So be optimistic and enjoy each stage of your life. It will keep you young for ever. It is you who will score more in every sphere of life.

Notes

Notes

Notes

Notes